SLIPPING THROUGH THE CRACKS

Unaccompanied Children Detained by the U.S. Immigration and Naturalization Service

Human Rights Watch Children's Rights Project

Human Rights Watch
New York · Washington · London · Brussels

ISBN 1-56432-209-2
Library of Congress Catalog Card Number: 97-71373

Human Rights Watch Childen's Rights Project
The Human Rights Watch Children's Rights Project was established in 1994 to monitor and promote the human rights of children around the world. Lois Whitman is the director; Yodon Thonden is counsel; Rosa Erenreich and Lee Tucker are consultants; and Linda Shipley is the associate. Jane Green Schaller is chair of the Advisory committee.

Addresses for Human Rights Watch
485 Fifth Avenue, New York, NY 10017-6104
Tel: (212) 972-8400, Fax: (212) 972-0905, E-mail: hrwnyc@hrw.org

1522 K Street, N.W., #910, Washington, DC 20005-1202
Tel: (202) 371-6592, Fax: (202) 371-0124, E-mail: hrwdc@hrw.org

33 Islington High Street, N1 9LH London, UK
Tel: (171) 713-1995, Fax: (171) 713-1800, E-mail: hrwatchuk@gn.apc.org

15 Rue Van Campenhout, 1000 Brussels, Belgium
Tel: (2) 732-2009, Fax: (2) 732-0471, E-mail: hrwatcheu@gn.apc.org

Web Site Address: http://www.hrw.org
Gopher Address://gopher.humanrights.org:5000/11/int/hrw
Listserv address: To subscribe to the list, send an e-mail message to majordomo@igc.apc.org with "subscribe hrw-news" in the body of the message (leave the subject line blank).

HUMAN RIGHTS WATCH

Human Rights Watch conducts regular, systematic investigations of human rights abuses in some seventy countries around the world. Our reputation for timely, reliable disclosures has made us an essential source of information for those concerned with human rights. We address the human rights practices of governments of all political stripes, of all geopolitical alignments, and of all ethnic and religious persuasions. Human Rights Watch defends freedom of thought and expression, due process and equal protection of the law, and a vigorous civil society; we document and denounce murders, disappearances, torture, arbitrary imprisonment, discrimination, and other abuses of internationally recognized human rights. Our goal is to hold governments accountable if they transgress the rights of their people.

Human Rights Watch began in 1978 with the founding of its Helsinki division. Today, it includes five divisions covering Africa, the Americas, Asia, the Middle East, as well as the signatories of the Helsinki accords. It also includes three collaborative projects on arms transfers, children's rights, and women's rights. It maintains offices in New York, Washington, Los Angeles, London, Brussels, Moscow, Dushanbe, Rio de Janeiro, and Hong Kong. Human Rights Watch is an independent, nongovernmental organization, supported by contributions from private individuals and foundations worldwide. It accepts no government funds, directly or indirectly.

The staff includes Kenneth Roth, executive director; Michele Alexander, development director; Cynthia Brown, program director; Holly J. Burkhalter, advocacy director; Barbara Guglielmo, finance and administration director; Robert Kimzey, publications director; Jeri Laber, special advisor; Lotte Leicht, Brussels office director; Susan Osnos, communications director; Jemera Rone, counsel; Wilder Tayler, general counsel; and Joanna Weschler, United Nations representative.

The regional directors of Human Rights Watch are Peter Takirambudde, Africa; José Miguel Vivanco, Americas; Sidney Jones, Asia; Holly Cartner, Helsinki; and Eric Goldstein, Middle East (acting). The project directors are Joost R. Hiltermann, Arms Project; Lois Whitman, Children's Rights Project; and Dorothy Q. Thomas, Women's Rights Project.

The members of the board of directors are Robert L. Bernstein, chair; Adrian W. DeWind, vice chair; Roland Algrant, Lisa Anderson, William Carmichael, Dorothy Cullman, Gina Despres, Irene Diamond, Fiona Druckenmiller, Edith Everett, Jonathan Fanton, James C. Goodale, Jack Greenberg, Vartan Gregorian, Alice H. Henkin, Stephen L. Kass, Marina Pinto Kaufman, Bruce Klatsky, Harold Hongju Koh, Alexander MacGregor, Josh Mailman, Samuel K. Murumba, Andrew Nathan, Jane Olson, Peter Osnos, Kathleen Peratis, Bruce Rabb, Sigrid Rausing, Anita Roddick, Orville Schell, Sid Sheinberg, Gary G. Sick, Malcolm Smith, Domna Stanton, Nahid Toubia, Maureen White, Rosalind C. Whitehead, and Maya Wiley.

ACKNOWLEDGMENTS

This report is based on research in California by Lee Tucker and Rosa Ehrenreich, consultants to the Children's Rights Project of Human Rights Watch, and on Lee Tucker's research in Arizona. The report was written by Rosa Ehrenreich and edited by Lee Tucker, Lois Whitman, the director of the Children's Rights Project, and Cynthia Brown, program director of Human Rights Watch. Other Human Rights Watch staff who offered helpful comments on the manuscript were Betsy Anderson, Dinah PoKempner, Allyson Collins, Alison Parker, and Linda Shipley.

We are grateful to the many individuals and organizations who helped to make this report possible. Immigration and Naturalization Services officials Alexander Aleinikoff, executive associate commissioner for programs; Ruben Cortines, director of detention management branch, Detention and Deportation Division; Elizabeth Herskovitz, detention and deportation officer; Ken Elwood, INS acting chief enforcement officer, Field Operations; and Joan Higgins, assistant commissioner, Detention and Deportation Branch, gave us essential background information and helped to facilitate our regional research. In California, we were assisted by Rosemary Melville and Leonard Kovensky, both of the Los Angeles District Office of the INS. Other INS staff members likewise helped facilitate our visit, as did Billy Burkette of the Los Angeles County Probation Department and the staff and management of the juvenile facilities at Eastlake, Sylmar and Los Padrinos. We are also indebted to the following individuals in Los Angeles's public-interest community: Judy London, Lorena Muñoz, Niels Frenzen, Gilbert Fung, Sharon Lowe, Carlos Holguin, Heidi Sanchez, Tim Everett and Vera Weisz, among others. In Arizona, we were aided immeasurably by the assistance of Gloria Goldman, Jennifer Huang, Patsy Kraeger, Deirdre Mokos, and other members of the immigration bar. From the Phoenix District of the INS we thank Bill Cravener, Pat Vroom, Annie López, and Jim Barrett, as well as the staff of the Southwest Key facility. We are indebted to Roy Petty and Hugo Ruiz for their generous assistance in Illinois. Finally, we would like to thank Mary Diaz and Wendy Young of the Women's Commission for Refugee Women and Children, and Annie Wilson and Susan Schmidt of the Lutheran Immigration and Refugee Service for their generous assistance.

Most of all, we thank the many detained children who shared their stories with us. To protect their privacy, their names have been changed in this report.

CONTENTS

I. SUMMARY

Children in INS detention are invisible: they have slipped through the cracks in America's legal system. They are arrested by the INS, detained in highly restrictive settings, and provided with little information about their legal rights and status. Unlike adults detained by the INS, unaccompanied children are not eligible for release after posting bond, and many them remain in detention for months on end, bewildered and frightened, denied meaningful access to attorneys and to their relatives. Ultimately, most of the children are deported. Because these children speak little or no English and are rarely aware of their rights under U.S. law, and because their relatives in the United States, if they have any, are frequently in the same plight, the children are extremely vulnerable. Since they are undocumented, often only the INS is aware of their whereabouts, and the INS has a lamentable history of refusing to cooperate with community groups and public interest immigration attorneys who might assist the children.

While conditions for children in INS detention vary greatly, they are typically extremely poor. This report discusses detention conditions in Los Angeles County and Arizona, and is based primarily upon site visits and interviews conducted by Human Rights Watch researchers in 1996. We found that in these places, conditions for children in INS detention violate the children's rights under international law, the U.S. Constitution, U.S. statutory provisions, INS regulations, and the terms of court orders binding on the INS.

Each year, thousands of children enter the United States illegally.[1] Some of the children come with parents or relatives, but most come alone[2]; some are refugees, fleeing persecution in their home countries, while others hope to find work and send money home to their poverty-stricken families.

When they reach the United States (usually with little money and no ability to speak or understand English), these children face an uncertain future.

---

[1] Human Rights Watch follows the U.N. Convention on the Rights of the Child in defining as a child any person under the age of eighteen. United Nations Convention on the Rights of the Child, G.A. Res. 44/25, November 20, 1989; entered into force September 2, 1990.

[2] According to the United Nations High Commissioner for Refugees, "An unaccompanied child is a person who is under the age of eighteen years, unless under the law applicable to the child, majority is attained earlier, and who is separated from both parents and is not being cared for by an adult who by law or custom has the responsibility to do so." U.N. High Commissioner for Refugees: Note on Policies and Procedures in dealing With Unaccompanied Children Seeking Asylum, Geneva, July 1996, p. 2.

Some manage to reach migrant labor communities or to find relatives already living in American cities, and they merge unnoticed into the American population, often becoming legal permanent residents in time. But many of these children are apprehended by the Immigration and Naturalization Service (INS), which in 1990 arrested 8,500 undocumented children, 70 percent of whom were unaccompanied by an adult guardian.[3]

Once in the hands of the INS, the children generally face deportation or exclusion proceedings, and most of the thousands of children arrested are either released to family members or expelled from the United States within a few days. But for a variety of reasons, some of the children are detained by the INS while their cases are pending; at any given time, over two hundred children are in longer-term INS custody.[4] Between October 7 and October 14, 1996, for instance, the INS reported that 241 children were in longer-term detention; 28 percent of those children were fifteen or under, and 5 percent were under ten. More than half of the children had been in detention for over a month, and 20 percent had been in detention for more than four months. Most of the children were from Central or South America, with 22 percent from China and 9 percent from other countries (primarily in Africa or the Indian subcontinent).[5]

Some of the detained children are seeking asylum in the United States. The INS practice of detaining juvenile asylum-seekers runs counter to international standards: the United Nations High Commissioner for Refugees recommends that asylum-seekers should not be detained,[6] and the United Nations Convention on the

---

[3] Figures are from *Flores v. Reno*, 113 S. Ct. 1439, 1443 (1993) (quoting INS brief). These statistics are now several years old. We repeatedly asked the INS for up to date and comprehensive statistics on the number of unaccompanied children apprehended annually, the number taken into custody for less than seventy-two hours, and the ultimate disposition of all apprehended children, but were told that no more recent statistics were available because the INS does not keep such records. Human Rights Watch interview with Elizabeth Herskovitz, INS detention and deportation officer in Washington, D.C., December 11, 1996.

[4] By "longer-term," we mean custody that lasts for more than seventy-two hours. The INS claims not to keep records on children detained for less than seventy-two hours.

[5] "Juvenile Report, 10/7/97 - 10/14/97," provided to us by the INS.

[6] UNHCR General Rule No. 2. General standards on the treatment of refugees were established by the 28th Session of the Executive Committee (EXCOM) of the UNHCR, and articulated in the UNHCR's Handbook on Procedures and Criteria for Determining

Rights of the Child similarly states that detention of children (whether asylum-seekers or migrants) should be used only as a measure of last resort.[7]

Unaccompanied children are too young to be released on their own recognizance. This means that children who have no close relatives in the United States remain in detention, under the legal guardianship of the INS.[8] This poses a troubling conflict of interest: the children are arrested, imprisoned, and frequently deported, all by the same agency that is charged with caring for them and protecting their legal rights. But the INS is subject to little meaningful outside monitoring and remains almost entirely unaccountable for violations of the children's rights. Many other nations solve this problem by separating the care-giving function from the prosecution function. In Britain, Canada, Denmark, and the Netherlands, for instance, unaccompanied children are placed in the custody of appropriate child welfare authorities while immigration officials assess the children's status.

In Los Angeles County, some juvenile INS detainees—those with previous contact with the juvenile justice system—are placed in one of several county prisons for convicted juvenile offenders. They are locked up and made to wear prison uniforms, although they are being detained for administrative reasons only: but for their INS status, they would be released. The children are given no personal privacy and cannot keep their personal possessions. In some facilities, they are illegally housed with the general prison population. Their access to counseling services and to recreational facilities is minimal. At an age when they should be in school, they are provided with few books, and those books are often in English, a language most of the children cannot read. Children are not permitted to leave the detention facilities except for court hearings, and on court dates they

---

Refugee Status. While the EXCOM Conclusions are non-binding international agreements, the handbook is accepted as the authoritative explanation of treaty standards.

[7] U.N. Convention on the Rights of the Child, Article 37.

[8] According to public interest attorneys, even children with relatives in the United States often experience difficulties rejoining their families after being detained by the INS, because the INS requires family members to provide information about their immigration status before initiating the release process. The INS has been unwilling to guarantee that it will not use this information to later apprehend and prosecute family members living illegally in the United States. As a result, many families are afraid to approach the INS to obtain the release of their detained children. Therefore, many children remain in INS detention in highly restrictive settings at significant expense to American taxpayers, despite the existence of family members willing and able to provide for their care.

are frequently transported to court in handcuffs, going without meals all day while waiting for their court appearances.

The children are given inadequate information about their legal rights, and frequently cannot obtain information in a language they understand. For non-Spanish speaking children, interpreters are rare to non-existent. Children are frequently transferred from one detention facility to another (sometimes in a different state) with no advance warning and no notice to their relatives or attorneys. Indeed, most of the children do not have attorneys. Children in detention have only limited access to telephones, and are sometimes denied the opportunity to speak privately with family members and legal representatives.

Conditions for juvenile INS detainees in Los Angeles County were the subject of a major class action suit brought in 1985. As a result of the litigation, the INS entered into a consent decree, agreeing to improve conditions nationwide and to keep all detained children in "non-secure" shelter care facilities befitting their status as non-criminal administrative detainees. (The INS defines "non-secure" facilities as facilities "without security fences or security hardware or other major construction typically associated with correctional facilities."[9]) Although some children remain in state juvenile detention facilities for convicted juvenile offenders, the INS has begun to place many children in privately operated shelter-care centers administered under contract with the INS. Unfortunately, conditions in some of the new shelter-care facilities are little better than in the county detention facilities.

In Arizona, for instance, children in INS custody are placed in a private secure facility in a remote town between Tucson and Phoenix. Children are not permitted to leave the grounds, which are surrounded by a tall wire fence, and may leave the locked building only under supervision. Many children have been confined to the facility for months without a single trip off the grounds, except for court hearings. The children live in crowded conditions, with very little free time, only one hour a day out of doors, and no personal privacy. Their access to reading materials is limited. These conditions violate INS regulations and the terms of the consent decree binding upon the INS, as well as international human rights standards.

---

[9] United States Department of Justice Community Relations Service, "Alien Minors Shelter Care Program, Program Guidelines and Requirements," p. 6. We were unable to obtain a date for this document, but an INS official told us that it was developed in 1995 to be given to all potential contracting agencies. Human Rights Watch Interview with Elizabeth Herskovitz, INS Detention and Deportation Officer, January 28, 1997.

In terms of access to legal representation, children in the Arizona facility fare even worse than their counterparts in Los Angeles County. To begin with, the region has few immigration attorneys who represent indigent clients. Furthermore, in blatant violation of the law, many children appear to receive no information about their right to be represented by an attorney, and the children are often denied the right to make telephone calls to their families or to attorneys. Local attorneys report difficulties in visiting the facility to contact clients, and the facility has repeatedly refused to permit legal service groups to make presentations to the children about their legal rights.

Overall, two factors combine to cause these inadequate detention conditions. First and foremost, the Immigration and Naturalization Service has consistently exhibited a combination of neglect and bad faith in dealing with the issue of children in detention. While there are undoubtedly numerous dedicated and conscientious individuals within the INS, many of the INS officials we encountered evidenced little concern for the rights of children. We encountered serious difficulties in obtaining accurate information about the number and status of children in INS detention, and, especially in Arizona, we had difficulty gaining access to detention facilities and getting permission to conduct confidential interviews with children. INS officials repeatedly contradicted themselves and gave us information that they knew or should have known to be false or misleading. Public interest attorneys report similar behavior from INS officials, and the testimony of the children we interviewed confirmed that INS officials and their agents were violating the law.

The problem is compounded by the dearth of funding for the provision of legal services to undocumented children. There has never been adequate *pro bono* legal assistance for juvenile INS detainees, and recent cuts in federal funding have worsened the situation. (In Los Angeles, for instance, virtually no one in the public interest legal community is currently able to represent indigent juvenile INS detainees.)

Furthermore, recent changes in the law prohibit all recipients of federal Legal Services Corporation funds from providing representation to undocumented aliens and from engaging in political activities or legislative lobbying. In consequence, although unaccompanied alien children are a uniquely vulnerable group, conditions for those children in INS detention are not adequately monitored or challenged. The INS thus remains free to violate children's rights in flagrant disregard of U.S. laws and international human rights standards.

Recommendations
Human Rights Watch recommends that the following steps be taken to ameliorate the situation:

Recommendations to the United States
- United States Attorney General Janet Reno and INS Commissioner Doris Meissner should order the INS to comply fully with all relevant national laws, regulations, and international standards concerning detention conditions for children.

- In particular, the U.S. government should work towards full compliance with the UNHCR Guidelines on Detention of Asylum Seekers, UNHCR Guidelines on the Protection and Care of Refugee Children, and the UNHCR Note on Policies and Procedures in Dealing with Unaccompanied Children Seeking Asylum.

- To prevent conflicts of interest, the same agency should not be charged both with the care-taking and the prosecution of unaccompanied, undocumented alien children. Once apprehended by the INS, unaccompanied children should be placed in the custody of appropriate child welfare authorities.

Detention Policies and Conditions
- Unaccompanied children awaiting determination of their status should not be detained.

- Until arrangements have been made to transfer custody of unaccompanied children from the INS to appropriate child welfare authorities:

- Attorney General Reno should order that the INS immediately cease to place detained unaccompanied children in state juvenile justice or criminal justice facilities, or in other facilities with prison-like conditions.

- In emergencies where there is no alternative to placing children in juvenile prisons, placement should be for the shortest possible period of time, and children should be separated from the ordinary prison population.

- Safety considerations may require keeping some children in secure facilities to protect them against recapture by smugglers. Such determinations should be made only on a case by case basis, however, and such children should be detained in secure facilities only if a thorough and individualized investigation reveals no possible safe alternatives.

- Shelter-care facilities should be in major ports of entry to the United States, and, when possible, children should be placed in shelter-care facilities in the area in which they were originally apprehended, or in which they have friends or relatives.

- Children in detention (whether in juvenile detention facilities or in private shelter-care facilities) should be permitted to retain their own clothes and personal belongings, receive an adequate education, to attend public school whenever possible, to visit public libraries, and to go on frequent educational and recreational field trips, as required by INS regulations.

- Children should be given unrestricted and private access to telephones and assisted in making calls. The INS should enable children to call relatives who cannot accept collect calls.

- The INS should investigate alternatives to detention and should develop a roster of local social service agencies willing to accept responsibility for an unaccompanied child's care, and/or a roster of foster families in the area in which the child was originally detained. The INS should develop such alternatives to detention with the assistance and approval of local public interest attorneys and community groups.

Access to Legal Information and Representation
- All unaccompanied children awaiting determination of their immigration status should have access to meaningful legal representation.

- No agency should receive a contract to provide shelter care for unaccompanied children unless it provides a full and complete plan for ensuring that all children in its facilities will have access to meaningful legal representation.

- The government should pay for independent legal representation for all unaccompanied children awaiting determination of their immigration status.

- Children should promptly and regularly receive information about their legal rights in a language they can understand, and they should be informed of all legally relevant information (court dates, etc.). They should also be informed both verbally and in writing of their right to contact the United Nations High Commissioner for Refugees.

- The INS should ensure that all written rights advisory forms are translated into the language spoken by each child.

- A sufficient number of trained interpreters should be provided at facilities housing unaccompanied children, as required by the shifting language populations in the facilities.

- The INS should keep children, their attorneys, and the local public interest bar informed of all legal and policy developments affecting the children.

Monitoring of Conditions and Practices
- The INS should keep statistics on all children apprehended and detained, including those detained for less than seventy-two hours and those who accept voluntary departure as an alternative to deportation proceedings. For those detained less than seventy-two hours, the following information should be recorded: place of apprehension; place and length of detention; whether the child was given the opportunity to call a parent, close relative or friend, or free legal services organization and whether such a call was in fact made; whether the child accepted voluntary departure, and, if voluntary departure was accepted, when, where, and to whom the child's custody was transferred. The INS should also maintain statistics of all children apprehended who do not accept voluntary departure, including the reasons for such decisions, i.e., the child proves she is legally in the country, the child asks to apply for political asylum, the child is eligible for adjustment of status, etc.

- The INS should keep accurate and comprehensive statistics on children in longer-term detention and their ultimate legal disposition. This information should be made available to the public.

- As long as the INS retains custody of unaccompanied children, each INS district should keep comprehensive statistics on the children's status, ensure that detention facilities provide appropriate standards of care, and maintain meaningful contact with children's attorneys and the immigration and public interest bars.

- In each INS region, an oversight committee should be formed to monitor conditions for detained children. Membership of the committee should include representatives of local social service and legal service groups, and the committee should be empowered to make spot inspections of all juvenile detention facilities and to recommend changes in placement options.

- No agency should receive a contract to provide shelter care for unaccompanied children unless it provides a full and complete plan for ensuring that all applicable laws, regulations, and standards will be complied with, including those found in the Justice Department's "Alien Minors Shelter Care Program, Program Guidelines and Requirements."

Recommendations to the United Nations High Commissioner for Refugees
The UNHCR should:
- Give priority to the needs of unaccompanied children, who are particularly vulnerable;

- Actively, extensively, and regularly investigate conditions in facilities in which unaccompanied children are detained to ensure that their treatment complies with international laws and standards and with UNHCR guidelines and policies; make its findings public;

- Pay particular attention to children's access to lawyers and interpreters, and to children's ability to contact family members or adult friends by telephone or otherwise;

- Talk with children privately and for whatever time is necessary to assess their situation and treatment;

- Request the U.S. Immigration and Naturalization Service to provide full information on the total number of unaccompanied children taken into custody, including those released or those who accept voluntary departure within seventy-two hours. This information should include the number, ages, and nationalities of the children; place of apprehension; place and length of detention; the number of children applying for asylum; the disposition of each case; when, where, and to whom each child was ultimately released; whether the children had access to legal representation, and the number of children who contacted family members or other adult friends;

• Meet regularly with nongovernmental organizations and lawyers' groups working actively on the issue of unaccompanied children and their treatment by the INS.

II. LEGAL BACKGROUND

The situation faced by unaccompanied minors is inherently coercive.
—Perez-Funez v. INS[10]

Unaccompanied minors apprehended by the INS have a number of options. If they don't wish to risk losing in a deportation hearing, they can accept "voluntary departure"; if they do this, they are permitted to leave the United States voluntarily, at their own expense and within a certain period of time. Accepting voluntary departure is legally more advantageous than deportation, because an alien who is deported for "entry without inspection" (i.e. illegal entry) develops a record that will hamper any future attempts to enter the United States through legal avenues. Allowing illegal entrants to depart voluntarily is also economically beneficial to the United States, since deportation, unlike voluntary departure, is at the expense of the U.S. government. As a result, minors apprehended by the INS are ordinarily offered voluntary departure immediately following their detention, and some unknown, but probably large, percentage of children, especially those from Mexico, accept this option.[11] Children who do not wish to accept voluntary departure, or who cannot afford to pay their own way home, may choose to admit deportability, and be sent home at the government's leisure and at government expense. Immigration judges cannot accept admissions of deportability from children under sixteen, however, unless they are represented by an attorney or accompanied by an adult friend, relative or legal guardian.[12]

Children who wish to remain in the United States may raise one of several defenses during deportation or exclusion hearings. Some children may have traveled to the United States simply to join family members who are U.S. citizens or legal residents. Children in this situation may petition for "adjustment of status" and permission to remain in the United States under the guardianship of their legally resident relative. But many children come to the United States to avoid persecution at home. These children can defend themselves against deportation or exclusion by making a political asylum claim, for a minor who can prove a well-

---

[10] *Perez-Funez v. INS*, 619 F. Supp. 656, 662 (C.D. Cal. 1985).

[11] The INS claims to keep no records on the number of minors accepting voluntary departure.

[12] 8 C.F.R. 242.16 (b).

11

founded fear of persecution at home will be granted permission to remain legally in the United States.[13] Some minors may also be able to remain in the U.S. by claiming "temporary protected status" if they come from a country declared by Congress to be dangerously unstable, whether because of civil strife, war or natural catastrophes such as earthquakes.[14] Finally, minors who are not fleeing from persecution and do not qualify for temporary protected status may, in some circumstances, qualify to remain in the United States as "special immigrants." This occasionally happens in the case of minors who have been away from their own country, and in the United States, for a long time, and who no longer have any family in their home country. These minors are declared wards of the court, and are placed by the state in foster care until the reach the age of majority.[15]

Deportation and exclusion hearings take place before immigration judges, and the INS is represented by trial attorneys. Raising any of the defenses discussed above is complex and sometimes costly: compiling persuasive evidence of a well-founded fear of persecution, for instance, may require extensive research and evidence-gathering. Unaccompanied minors are very poorly equipped to get through the legal process. Even most American-born children normally have only a vague grasp of the legal process, and foreign-born children—often with little education—find the process even more bewildering, since it is conducted using rules they don't know, and in a language they cannot understand. This makes it virtually impossible for children without lawyers to prevail in deportation or exclusion hearings.

Because of the uniquely vulnerable situation of unaccompanied migrant, asylum-seeker, and other undocumented children, both the international community and the United States have developed laws and guidelines aimed at protecting their rights and welfare.

---

[13] Immigrants will not be deported if they can demonstrate that they left their home country out of a well-founded fear of persecution for reasons of race, religion, political opinion or membership in a particular social group. 8 U.S.C.S. 1253.

[14] As of February 1997, citizens of Rwanda, Liberia, Somalia and Bosnia are eligible to apply for temporary protected status.

[15] 8 C.F.R. 101.6

International Standards for Children in Confinement

Numerous United Nations documents lay out guidelines that affect unaccompanied minors in INS detention. The U.N. Convention on the Rights of the Child,[16] the U.N. Rules for Juveniles Deprived of their Liberty,[17] and the U.N. High Commissioner for Refugees' Note on Policies and Procedures in dealing with Unaccompanied Children Seeking Asylum[18] are among the most salient international documents. (See appendix for the text of these documents). These agreements and documents clearly establish minimum international standards for the fair and humane treatment of children in INS detention. The United Nations High Commissioner for Refugees is responsible for supervising states' compliance with the United Nations Convention Relating to the Status of Refugees. To that end, these documents require states to cooperate with the UNHCR.[19]

---

[16] United Nations Convention on the Rights of the Child. Signed by the Clinton administration in February 1995; as of February 1997 the Convention has not been ratified by the United States Senate.

[17] G.A. Res. 45/113, April 2, 1991.

[18] U.N. High Commissioner for Refugees' Note on Policies and Procedures in dealing with Unaccompanied Children Seeking Asylum, Geneva, July 1996. (Hereafter "Note on Policies.")

[19] The United Nations Convention relating to the Status of Refugees was adopted by the United Nations in 1951, and entered into force in 1954. In Article 35, the Convention States:
1.   The Contracting States undertake to co-operate with the Office of the United Nations High Commissioner for Refugees, or any other agency of the United Nations which may succeed it, in the exercise of its functions, and shall in particular facilitate its duty of supervising the application of the provisions of the Convention.
2.   In order to enable the Office of the High Commissioner or any other agency of the United Nations which may succeed it, to make reports to the competent organs of the United Nations, the Contracting States undertake to provide them in the appropriate form with information and statistical data requested concerning:
(a) The condition of refugees,
(b) The implementation of this Convention, and
(c) Laws, regulations, and decrees which are, or may hereafter be, in force relating to refugees.
The United Nations Protocol relating to the Status of Refugees which entered into force in 1967, contains essentially identical language in Article II.

In general, international guidelines establish the following rights relating to legal representation:

•   Detained minors have a right to contact and receive visits from friends, relatives, and legal counsel.

•   Detained minors must be helped to understand their rights.

•   All detained minors have a right to prompt legal assistance.

•   Legal procedures should be prompt, expeditious and at no cost for detained persons without adequate means.[20]

International guidelines also establish minimum standards relating to confinement conditions:

•   Unaccompanied children seeking asylum should not be detained.[21]

---

[20]Note on Policies, Sections 5.7, 5.14, 8.2, 8.3. See also Guidelines 4, 5, and 6 (ii). The UNHCR Note on Policies and Procedures also recommends that unaccompanied detained minors should have appointed legal guardians: "It is suggested that an independent and formally accredited organization be identified/established in each country, which will appoint a guardian or adviser as soon as the unaccompanied child is identified." Note on Policies, Sections 5.7.

As mentioned in the recommendation section to this report, Human Rights Watch believes that to prevent conflicts of interest, unaccompanied children apprehended by the INS should be placed in the custody of appropriate child welfare authorities, rather than in facilities operated by—or under contract to—the INS. At least until such time as this recommendation is adopted by the United States government, however, Human Rights Watch shares the UNHCR's view that each detained unaccompanied child should have an independent legal guardian appointed to represent the child's best interests, which may be contrary to the interests of the INS. It should be emphasized that a legal guardian is not a substitute for an attorney. Children with appointed guardians continue to require attorneys to represent them in their deportation or exclusion hearings.

[21] Note on Policies, 7.6; see also Guideline 5.

- If detention occurs it should be a measure of last resort and for the shortest appropriate period of time.[22]

- The best interests of the minor should be a primary consideration.[23]

- Detained juvenile asylum-seekers should not be held in prison-like conditions.[24]

- Detention should only be in facilities guaranteeing meaningful activities and programs promoting the development and health of the young person.[25]

- All efforts must be made to have the children released from detention.[26]

- Minors in detention have a right to education, medical treatment, exercise and recreation facilities.[27]

- Detained minors must be held separately from unrelated adults.[28]

- Detained minors are entitled to a reasonable degree of personal privacy.[29]

---

[22] Note on Policies, 7.7; see also U.N. Convention on the Rights of the Child (Hereafter C.R.C.), Art. 37, and U.N. Rules for Juveniles Deprived of their Liberty (Hereafter "Rules"), I. 2.

[23] U.N. C.R.C, Art. 3 (1).

[24] Note, 7.8.

[25] Rules, II.. 12.

[26] Guidelines, Guideline 5.

[27] See C.R.C, Notes, Guidelines, Rules, infra.

[28] Guidelines, Guideline 6.

[29] Rules 4. D. 31.

United States Legal Standards for Minors in INS Detention
Rights of Aliens In General

The United States Supreme Court has long recognized that most constitutional provisions are applicable to non-citizens, including those who illegally enter the United States. In *Shaughnessy v. United States*, the court insisted that aliens are entitled to due process before being deported: "Aliens who have once passed through our gates, even illegally, may be expelled only after proceedings conforming to traditional standards of fairness encompassed in due process of law."[30] In *Plyler v. Doe*, the court reaffirmed its commitment to protecting the rights of aliens: "Whatever his status under the immigration laws, an alien is surely a 'person' in any ordinary sense of that term. Aliens, even aliens whose presence in this country is unlawful, have long been recognized as 'persons' guaranteed due process of law by the Fifth and Fourteenth Amendments."[31]

Rights of Children in General

In the United States, children have the same basic right to constitutional protection as adults, as the U.S. Supreme Court noted in the 1967 landmark case *In re Gault*: "Neither the Fourteenth Amendment nor the Bill of Rights is for adults only."[32] In 1979, the court reaffirmed this principle in *Bellotti v. Baird*: "[A] child, merely on account of his minority, is not beyond the protection of the Constitution."[33]

In *Bellotti*, the Supreme Court was careful to point out that in addition to their basic constitutional rights, children may require additional legal protection: "As Mr. Justice Frankfurter aptly put it: '[C]hildren have a very special place in life which law should reflect. . . .[C]onstitutional principles [must] be applied with sensitivity and flexibility to the special needs of parents and children. . . . [While] children generally are protected by the same guarantees against government

---

[30] *Shaughnessy v. U.S.*, 206 U.S. 206, 212 (1953).

[31] *Plyler v. Doe*, 457 U.S. 202, 210 (1981).

[32] *In re Gault*, 387 U.S. 1, 13 (1967).

[33] *Bellotti v. Baird*, 443 U.S. 622, 633 (1979).

deprivation as are adults, the State is entitled to adjust its legal system to account for children's vulnerability.'"[34]

There are only a few cases that deal specifically with the issues faced by unaccompanied children detained by the INS. But despite the relative dearth of case law, several federal courts have recognized the inherent vulnerability of children in INS custody. In *Perez-Funez v. INS*, for instance, a federal trial court in California found that the INS had violated the due process rights of unaccompanied minors by forcing them to accept voluntary departure from the United States (thus waiving their right to a hearing before an immigration judge) without their effective knowledge or consent. The *Perez-Funez* court noted that "the situation faced by unaccompanied minors is inherently coercive."[35]

Official INS regulations also acknowledge that the rights of children require special protection. Thus, the INS is normally required to notify a child's parent or guardian promptly if a child is apprehended. [36] The regulations also state

---

[34] *Bellotti*, at 634, 635, quoting *May v. Anderson*, 345 U.S. 528, 536. (1953) (concurring opinion).

[35] *Perez Funez v. INS*, 619 F. Supp. 656, 662 (C.D. Cal. 1985). The *Perez-Funez* court issued a nationally applicable injunction requiring the INS to ensure that unaccompanied minors have adequate opportunity to consult with an adult before signing a voluntary departure form: "With respect to class members apprehended in the immediate vicinity of the border and who reside permanently in Mexico or Canada, the INS shall inform the class member that he or she may make a telephone call to a parent, close relative or friend, or to an organization found on the free legal services list. The INS shall so inform the class member of this opportunity prior to presentation of the voluntary departure form. . . . With respect to all other class members, the INS shall provide access to telephones and shall ensure that the class member has in fact communicated, by telephone or otherwise, with a parent, close adult relative or friend, or with an organization found on the free legal service list. The INS shall provide such access and ensure communication prior to presentation of the voluntary departure form." P. 670.

[36] When the INS locates someone it believes to be an illegal alien, the first step in initiating deportation proceedings is normally the issuance of an "Order to Show Cause" (O.S.C.). Essentially, the O.S.C. informs the suspected illegal alien that s/he will be deported unless s/he can "show cause" for remaining in the country: i.e., the suspected alien must raise some defense to deportation or exclusion (for instance, by raising an asylum defense, or petitioning for adjustment of status). According to the regulations, in the case of a deportable child of fourteen or under, the Order to Show Cause must be served upon the "person with whom the minor resides," and "whenever possible" also upon the minor's nearest relative or guardian. 8 C.F.R. 242.3 (a) and 8 C.F.R. 103.5a(c)(2).

that an immigration trial judge "shall not accept an admission of deportability from an unrepresented respondent who is . . . under age sixteen and is not accompanied by a guardian, relative or close friend."[37] This regulation is of particular importance, since unrepresented minors are often unaware of the option of applying for asylum, temporary protected status or special immigrant status. Far from family and friends, without access to legal counsel, and going through highly technical legal hearings conducted in a foreign language, these children may admit deportability in court only because they do not realize that they have other legal options. INS regulations such as this accord with the general judicial recognition that children are unusually vulnerable, and may be unable to understand fully the ramifications of their legal situation without adult assistance.[38]

---

[37] 8 C.F.R. 242.16

[38] Congress, too, has shown a long-standing concern for the vulnerability of children caught up in the legal system. The Federal Juvenile Delinquency Act is one of many examples of the Congressional intent to protect the rights of children. The F.J.D.A. provides juveniles with some statutory protections beyond those offered to adults: for instance, the F.J.D.A. requires arresting officers to "immediately advise [an arrested] juvenile of all his legal rights, in a language comprehensible to a juvenile." The arresting officer must also notify the juvenile's parents or guardian. 18 U.S.C.S. 5033. Although minors in INS detention are essentially administrative detainees, held by the INS only because the INS believes there to be no suitable release option available, it is arguably the case that many of the statutory protections created by the F.J.D.A. apply to them. This is because the F.J.D.A. provides these protections to juveniles "taken into custody for an alleged act of juvenile delinquency," and the F.J.D.A. defines juvenile delinquency as the "violation of a law of the United States committed by a person prior to his eighteenth birthday which would have been a crime if committed by an adult." (18 U.S.C.S. 5031) Since entry without inspection can constitute a federal crime if committed by an adult (8 U.S.C.S. 1325), juveniles taken into custody by INS officers may be covered by the F.J.D.A..

Two Ninth Circuit decisions have noted that "the Federal Juvenile Delinquency Act applies to aliens as well as to American Citizens. . ." Even if the juvenile is an illegal entrant into this country and his parents reside abroad, the Government must make reasonable efforts to notify the parent." *United States v. Doe*, 862 F. 2d. 776 (9th Cir. 1988).

The Ninth Circuit has also held that in cases of conflict between INS regulations and provisions of the F.J.D.A., the F.J.D.A. is controlling. See *United States v. Doe*, 701 F. 2d. 819, 822 (9th Cir. 1983).

Right to Counsel

In general, deportable aliens are entitled to counsel of their own choosing and at their own expense.[39] Excludable aliens are entitled to counsel if they file asylum claims as defenses in exclusion proceedings.[40] Although the government has no statutory obligation to appoint legal counsel for aliens who cannot afford their own lawyer, INS officials and immigration judges must inform aliens of their right to counsel and of the existence of free legal services provided by external groups such as legal aid organizations or pro bono lawyers' associations.[41]

Federal courts have taken the issue of the right to counsel extremely seriously: for instance, in *Orantes-Hernandez v. Meese*, a federal trial court observed that since aliens have both statutory and constitutional rights to a representative of their choosing, any INS regulations or practices that obstruct the right to counsel are invalid. The *Orantes* court went even further, however, noting that INS "detention officials must not only refrain from placing obstacles in the way of communication between detainees and their attorneys, but are obligated to affirmatively provide detainees with legal assistance."[42]

---

[39] 8 U.S.C.S. 1252, 1362.

[40] An alien who has entered the United States is deportable; aliens who are apprehended at the border are excludable. Aliens detained within the United States for the sole purpose of determining their excludability are not considered to have "entered" the United States—thus, aliens apprehended while trying to pass through airport immigration control may be detained at a facility in the United States, but legally they are not considered to have "entered" the U.S., and are thus subject to exclusion proceedings rather than deportation proceedings. Aliens who have effected an entry into the U.S. have a wider range of due process rights than excludable aliens. As a result, the discussion that follows focuses primarily on children in deportation proceedings. Nonetheless, Human Rights Watch believes that the Fifth Amendment due process clause obligates the government to provide both deportable and excludable children with government-appointed counsel. In our view, the absence of attorneys for children in either sort of proceeding constitutes a denial of fundamental fairness.

[41] INS regulations require INS officers to inform aliens of their right to counsel at no expense to the government at the time the Order to Show Cause is served, and require immigration judges to repeat this information to aliens who come before them. 8 C.F.R 242.1

[42] *Orantes-Hernandez v. Meese*, 685 F. Supp. 1488, 1510 (C.D. Cal. 1988), aff'd. sub. nom. *Orantes Hernandez v. Thornburgh*, 919 F. 2d. 549 (9th Cir. 1990). The *Orantes* Court found that the INS had violated the rights of detained aliens by unduly

Statutory provisions only entitle aliens to counsel at no expense to the government. However, there is a strong constitutional basis for asserting that the government has an obligation to provide counsel at government expense for indigent detained children going through deportation or exclusion proceedings. This issue has not been directly addressed by U.S. courts. But here too, what little case law there is provides support for the view that detained children who cannot afford a lawyer have a constitutional right to government-appointed counsel.

The Fifth and Fourteenth Amendments to the United States Constitution prohibit the federal and state governments from denying liberty to any person without due process of law.[43] Based on these due process guarantees, the Supreme Court held, in *Gideon v. Wainwright*, that the government must provide free counsel for indigent criminal defendants.[44] In *In re Gault*, the court went further and held that due process requires the government to provide lawyers for indigent children in juvenile delinquency proceedings, even though these proceedings are technically civil, rather than criminal, in nature. The Court based its holding in *Gault* on the fact that children in juvenile delinquency proceedings have a strong liberty interest at stake.[45]

---

restricting visits from attorneys and paralegals, failing to provide adequate telephone facilities and failing to provide adequate access to telephones. The Court also found that the INS was in violation of previous court orders and its own regulations by failing to provide detainees with accurate and complete lists of free legal service providers. These findings led the district court to issue a permanent injunction against INS practices obstructing the right to counsel, and the injunction was upheld by the Ninth Circuit Court of Appeals.

[43] The Fifth Amendment to the United States Constitution states: "No person shall . . . be deprived of life, liberty or property, without due process of law." United States Constitution, Amendment 5. The Fourteenth Amendment to the Constitution, which covers the actions of state governments, provides: "No state shall . . . deprive any person of life, liberty, or property, without due process of law." United States Constitution, Amendment 14.

[44] *Gideon v. Wainwright*, 372 U.S. 335 (1963).

[45] *In re Gault*, 387 U.S. 1 (1967) The Supreme Court held in *Gault* that "The Due Process clause of the Fourteenth Amendment requires that in respect of proceedings to determine delinquency which may result in commitment in an institution in which the juvenile's freedom of liberty is curtailed, the child and his parents must be notified of the child's right to be represented by counsel retained by them, or if they are unable to afford counsel, that counsel will be appointed to represent the child."(P.46). In the wake of *Gault*,

Like juvenile delinquency proceedings, deportation and exclusion proceedings are civil in nature, not criminal. Several courts have noted, however, that the consequences of a deportation proceeding are as grave as the consequences of many criminal proceedings, and a liberty interest is similarly at stake: thus, in *Brancato v. Lehmann*, the Sixth Circuit Court of Appeals observed that "although it is not penal in character, deportation is a drastic measure, at times the equivalent of banishment or exile. . ."[46] More recently, a Fifth Circuit case, *Johns v. Department of Justice*, noted that "deportation is not a criminal action, but the consequences may more seriously affect the deportee than a jail sentence. The liberty of the individual is at stake and 'meticulous care must be exercised lest the procedure by which he is deprived of that liberty not meet the essential standard of fairness.'"[47]

Two federal courts have commented directly on the issue of whether indigent aliens in deportation proceedings have a right to counsel at government expense, and have noted that when an alien's rights would be substantially impaired in the absence of counsel, the government may be constitutionally required to pay for the alien's counsel. In *Escobar-Ruiz v. INS*, the Ninth Circuit observed that "Congress' treatment of indigent aliens [in refusing to provide government-funded counsel] may not be constitutional as applied in individual cases. The Fifth Amendment guarantee of due process applies to immigration proceedings, and in specific proceedings, due process could be held to require that an indigent alien should be provided with counsel. . . ."[48] The Sixth Circuit reached a similar decision in *Aguilera-Enriquez v. INS*, stating that "where an unrepresented indigent alien would require counsel to present his position adequately to an

---

it seems clear the right to government-provided counsel rests not upon whether a proceeding is civil or criminal in nature, but upon the seriousness of the proceeding's consequences, and in particular, whether there are important constitutionally recognized interests at stake. See *Aguilere-Enriquez v INS*, 516 F. 2d. 565, note 3. (6th Cir. 1975).

[46] U.S. ex. rel. *Brancato v. Lehmann*, 239 F. 2d. 663, 666 (6th Cir. 1956).

[47] *Johns v. Dept. of Justice of the United States*, 624 F. 2d. 522, 524 (5th. Cir. 1980). The *Johns* court held that minors in deportation hearings may be entitled to the appointment of a guardian ad litem to represent their interests.

[48] *Escobar-Ruiz v. INS*, 787 F. 2d. 1294, 1297, note 3 (9th Cir. 1986), aff'd. 838 F. 2d. 1020 (9th Cir. 1988).

immigration judge he must be provided with a lawyer at the Government's expense. Otherwise, 'fundamental fairness' would be violated."[49]

If there is a strong argument for asserting that the government may, at times, be required by the constitution to provide legal counsel for indigent adult aliens in deportation proceedings, the argument is still stronger as it applies to unaccompanied minors.[50] Sitting *en banc*, the Ninth Circuit affirmed *Escobar v. Ruiz* and noted that "deportation proceedings are difficult for aliens to fully comprehend, let alone conduct, and individuals subject to such proceedings frequently require the assistance of counsel."[51] If the proceedings are difficult for adults to comprehend or conduct, they are nearly impossible for children: as the Court in *Perez-Funez* observed, unaccompanied children in INS custody "encounter a stressful situation in which they are forced to make critical decisions. Their interrogators are foreign and authoritarian. The environment is new and the culture completely different. The law is complex.... In short, it is obvious to the Court that the situation faced by unaccompanied minors is inherently coercive."[52]

Human Rights Watch confirmed the *Perez-Funez* court's observations in the facilities we visited. We found that unaccompanied children in INS detention are routinely held in conditions that violate their statutory rights. Often, the children are not informed of their rights, and to the extent that they receive legal information, it is frequently in a language that they cannot read or understand, and it is often incomplete or misleading. Far from family and friends, surrounded by strangers, the children are expected to negotiate their way through a foreign and bewilderingly complex legal process. But without legal counsel, detained minors have no ability to obtain legal relief if detention conditions violate their constitutional or statutory rights, and they have equally little chance of successfully asserting legitimate legal defenses to deportation or exclusion. Thus, Human Rights Watch believes that the due process clause of the Fifth Amendment requires the

---

[49] *Aguilere-Enriquez v. INS*, 516 F. 2d. 565, 568, note 3 (6th Cir. 1975).

[50] Arguably, the Federal Juvenile Delinquency Act applies to detained minors in deportation proceedings, and provides additional support for the view that such minors are entitled to government-appointed counsel: the F.J.D.A. states that "the juvenile shall be assisted by counsel during the transfer hearing, and at every other critical stage of the proceeding." 18 U.S.C.S. 5032.

[51] *Escobar-Ruiz v. INS*, 838 F. 2d. 1020, 1026 (9th Cir. 1988).

[52] *Perez-Funez v. INS*, 619 F. Supp. 656, 662 (C.D. Cal. 1985).

United States government to provide counsel to indigent unaccompanied children who have been detained by the INS pending the outcome of deportation or exclusion hearings.[53]

Release Options and Detention Conditions for Unaccompanied Minors

The INS has broad discretion to detain non-citizens who are apprehended while attempting to enter the U.S. illegally, or who are apprehended after entry into the United States. But according to the INS regulations, as interpreted by the Board of Immigration Appeals, "an alien generally . . . should not be detained or required to post bond except on a finding that he is a threat to the national security . . . or that he is a poor bail risk."[54] In the case of unaccompanied minors, the situation is somewhat more complicated, because "the INS cannot simply send [juveniles] off into the night on bond or recognizance."[55] Children require a responsible adult to care for them.

Until the early 1980s, there was no codified INS policy governing the detention and release of unaccompanied minors. Some regional INS offices would release minors only to parents, while other offices would release children to any responsible adult or organization. In 1984, the INS Western Region, which consists of Washington, Oregon, California, Arizona, Nevada, Hawaii, and Alaska, adopted a policy stating that except in "unusual and extraordinary cases," minors

---

[53] U.S. courts have found aliens in exclusion proceedings to be entitled to a narrower range of due process protections than aliens in deportation proceedings. But, for children especially, the outcome of exclusion proceedings, like the outcome of deportation proceedings, implicates a serious liberty interest. Like deportable children, excludable unaccompanied children may be detained within the United States for months, and if they do not prevail in their exclusion hearings, they may be returned to countries in which they face persecution. Without the assistance of attorneys, excludable children may not even realize that they can raise an asylum defense, much less have a chance of prevailing in the exclusion hearing. Thus, we believe that the extreme vulnerability of unaccompanied children, combined with the potentially grave consequences of exclusion hearings, give indigent excludable children a due process right to a government-appointed attorney.

The government should continue to pay for such counsel until the children have exhausted all appeal rights and/or have been released from detention into the custody of a family member, legal guardian or other responsible adult able to assume financial responsibility for the child's care.

[54] Quoted in *Flores v. Reno*, 113 S.Ct. 1429, 1143 (1993).

[55] Ibid.

would be released only to parents or legal guardians. In practice, this led to the detention of many more minors, since few minors could locate adults satisfying the Western Region's stringent requirement. Children not released were placed in a variety of INS detention facilities, usually in state and county juvenile prisons.[56]

Conditions for detained children in the Western Region were egregious enough to prompt a class action suit, initiated in 1985. The suit, which ultimately became known as *Flores v. Reno*,[57] challenged both the region's blanket detention policy for minors and the prison-like detention conditions. The suit resulted in two changes. First, the INS instituted a national policy governing the detention and release of unaccompanied minors. The changed policy, which applies to all INS branches nationwide, says that unaccompanied minors can be released to a parent, legal guardian or close adult relative, or to an unrelated adult designated by the minor's parents. In such cases, the minor's parents must execute "a sworn affidavit before an immigration officer or consular officer," stating that the designated adult is "capable and willing to care for the juvenile's well-being."[58] In the absence of such an affidavit, and in "unusual and compelling circumstances and in the discretion of the district director," an unaccompanied minor may be released to any adult who executes an agreement to care for the child and ensure his or her presence at immigration proceedings.[59]

This INS policy governing the release of unaccompanied minors was upheld by the Supreme Court, which stated, however, that the INS has no constitutional obligation to release detained minors, as long as detention conditions are adequate.[60] What constitutes "adequate" detention conditions has not been examined by the court, however, because the other change in INS policy brought about by the *Flores* suit was a settlement agreement governing detention conditions. The 1987 consent decree, administered by the district court for the Central District of California, obliges the INS to place detained minors in non-

---

[56] Ibid.

[57] *Flores v. Reno*, 113 S.Ct. 1429 (1993). The suit was originally filed as *Flores v. Meese*, since Edwin Meese was U.S. attorney general in 1985.

[58] 8 C.F.R. 242.24.

[59] 8 C.F.R. 242.24(4).

[60] *Flores v. Reno*, 113 S.Ct .1429, 1143 (1993).

secure shelter-care settings, rather than in juvenile prisons.[61] The consent decree forbids the INS from holding children in county detention facilities for more than seventy-two hours, except in emergencies, and lays out a detailed series of requirements for detention facilities (known as the "*Flores* requirements"). While the terms of the consent decree apply only to the Western Region of the INS, the INS adopted most of the *Flores* requirements as national policy. [62]

The INS has attempted to meet the *Flores* requirements by contracting with private and non-profit organizations to provide shelter-care facilities for detained minors. According to the regulations for the "Alien Minors Shelter Care Program," these contracting facilities must meet or exceed state licensing requirements, and must "[deliver services] in an open type of setting, i.e., without security fences and security hardware or other major restraining construction typically associated with correctional facilities." Facilities must deliver services "in a manner which is sensitive to culture, native language and the complex needs of these minors."[63]

Like international standards and U.S. case law and statutes, the INS regulations for the Alien Minor Shelter Care Program reflect an awareness of the vunerability of unaccompanied alien children. The regulations require that facilities provide minors with "an integrated and structured daily routine which shall include, but not be limited to: education, recreation, vocational experience or chores, study period, counseling, group interaction, free time and access to legal or religious services." Specifically, the regulations also provide that:

• "Program rules and disciplinary procedures must be written and translated into . . . a language understood by the minor. These rules must be provided to each minor and fully understood by each minor."

---

[61] The *Flores* court refused to hear findings on INS detention conditions, because of the consent decree: "There is, in short, no constitutional need for a hearing to determine whether private placement would be better, as long as institutional custody is (as we readily find it to be, assuming compliance with the requirements of the consent decree) good enough." *Flores*, p. 1449.

[62] The *Flores* requirements are laid out in detail in the Alien Minors Shelter Care Program, Program Guidelines and Requirements, U.S. Department of Justice, Community Relations Service.

[63] Ibid., p. 6.

- "Each minor is to enjoy a reasonable right to privacy."

- Facility staff must provide minors with "information regarding the availability of free legal assistance . . . the right to be represented by counsel at no expense to the government . . . the right to a deportation or exclusion hearing before an immigration judge . . . [and] that they may apply for political asylum or request voluntary departure in lieu of deportation."

- Staff at facilities "shall assist minors in making confidential contact with attorneys and their authorized representatives. An accurate and current reference list of voluntary agencies and attorneys who provide services without compensation will be posted and provided to all minors."

- Facility staff must ensure that minors have the opportunity to go on frequent field trips: "All minors shall be afforded opportunities for escorted visits to the surrounding communities for leisure activities at least twice each week." Staff must also respect the religious needs of minors: "Whenever possible, minors are to be afforded access to religious services of their choice." [64]

Our investigation revealed consistent and widespread violations of all of these regulations.

---

[64] Ibid., pp. 9-11, 18-24.

III. ACCESS TO LEGAL INFORMATION AND TO REPRESENTATION

Although children in INS detention have a clear right to be provided with adequate legal information and to be represented effectively by counsel of their own choosing, we were informed by numerous public interest lawyers and by an immigration judge that the majority of children receive minimal legal information and are unrepresented. Our interviews with children confirmed these reports. The lack of adequate information and representation makes a mockery of due process protections and leaves hundreds of children languishing for months in sub-standard detention conditions, bewildered and afraid, while their cases move slowly through the immigration courts. Hundreds more children are deported or accept voluntary departure, despite having what public interest attorneys say are viable asylum claims. "Kids who are waifs, who don't have anyone, will get whisked away, deported," one public interest lawyer told us. "The kids with good lawyers often get to stay. It has little to do with the merits of the case."[65]

The lack of trained immigration lawyers able to accept indigent clients is one reason so many children are unrepresented, but the INS also bears a substantial portion of the blame for detaining the children in conditions which make it overwhelmingly difficult for the children to have access to meaningful legal representation.

Los Angeles County

At any one time, the Los Angeles District of the INS normally has about twenty or thirty minors in detention.[66] Until the early spring of 1996, these children were placed in one of three county juvenile detention facilities: Eastlake, Los Padrinos or Sylmar. In late March, the INS began to transfer most minors to the new contract "shelter-care" facility in Arizona. However, the INS continues to detain many minors in Los Angeles County facilities for short periods of time, and minors deemed by the INS to be a security risk will continue to be held in Los Angeles County.

The procedures used by the INS to determine whether a minor requires detention in a secured facility seem arbitrary; at no time was a formal policy

---

[65] Human Rights Watch interview with Judy London, Central American Resource Center (CARECEN), April 22, 1996.

[66] Human Rights Watch interview with Rosemary Melville, INS Acting District Director for Los Angeles, April 18, 1996.

articulated to us. Apparently, any child who had come into contact with the criminal justice system, no matter how fleeting and trivial the contact, would be deemed a security risk. None of the children we met in Los Angeles County facilities would have been in detention, but for their INS status.

Nor would the INS guarantee that Los Angeles County juvenile detention centers will not be used more extensively in the future. When we met with the INS acting district director in Los Angeles, we expressed our concern about the process by which children were being transferred to Arizona. Although we had also told her of the inadequate detention conditions in Los Angeles, her sole response to our worries about transfer policies was to say, "we could move them back [to the county facilities]."[67] Thus, conditions for children apprehended in Los Angeles and detained in county facilities continue to be a problem of pressing concern.

When children are apprehended by the INS in Los Angeles, they are normally brought to the basement of the Federal Building, which serves as a "staging area." Better known as "B-18," the staging area consists of a large central room containing cubicles for INS officers, with "pods," or short-term detention cells, radiating off the side corridors. The "pods" are locked from the outside, and each pod contains unpadded benches against the walls, one pay telephone, and a small toilet stall with no door. The larger pods may contain several dozen detainees at one time. In general, detainees are placed into pods based on age, gender and language group. When we visited B-18, we were not permitted inside any of the occupied pods, because INS District Counsel John Salter told us that he "could not guarantee our safety,"[68] although the pods contained only non-criminal detainees. As a result, we were unable to see whether the legally-required information pertaining to free legal service groups was properly posted in each pod. We were also unable to make sure that the telephones were working. We were permitted only to look through the windows, and we were not allowed to speak to any of the detainees.

Although B-18 serves as the sole staging area in Los Angeles, INS officials could not or would not tell us whether all children apprehended in the Los Angeles region come through B-18. They told us that they do not keep statistics on the number of minors processed monthly or yearly in B-18, nor statistics on the disposition of each case (i.e., the number of minors released to relatives, the

---

[67] Human Rights Watch interview with Rosemary Melville, INS Acting District Director for Los Angeles, April 25, 1996.

[68] Human Rights Watch interview with John Salter, INS District Counsel for Los Angeles, April 23, 1996.

number accepting voluntary departure, the number sent to county facilities, and the number ultimately deported).[69] They also were unable or unwilling to tell us what steps each arrested minor would go through before release or detention.

We toured B-18 with INS Acting Assistant District Director Leonard Kovensky, District Counsel John Salter, and the head of the staging area, Narcisco Leggs, who also serves as the district's juvenile coordinator. Despite the presence of these high-level INS officials, when we asked how the INS ensured that minors actually contacted their relatives or lawyers before receiving voluntary departure forms (as required under the terms of the *Perez-Funez* court order), no one was able to tell us. We then asked what written information was provided to minors about their legal rights. No one was certain. When a shelf of forms was eventually found, none of the INS officials seemed clear which form was used for which purpose.

We eventually located the Spanish version of the form that minors must sign pursuant to the court order in *Perez-Funez v. INS*, stating that they have read and understood their rights to contact their relatives, speak to a lawyer and have a hearing before a judge. However, the box next to the line "He leido este aviso" ("I have read this notice") had been *pre-checked* on all the copies of the form. When we pointed this out to Mr. Salter, the district counsel, he at first told us that the form was pre-checked "to save time." He then suggested that it might be accidental, but that either way it was of little import because "maybe we don't give [the minors] those forms anyway." Needless to say, in either case this represents a violation of the minors' due process rights.

None of the legally-required forms—including the list of free legal service providers—had been translated into any language other than Spanish, despite the fact that many of the juveniles and adults processed in B-18 speak neither English nor Spanish (a significant number are Chinese). We asked how the INS ensures that minors understand their rights and were informed that when no interpreter is available to explain the forms, the INS makes use of the AT&T interpreter service, through which interpreters are provided by telephone. Children who speak "unusual" languages thus must depend on a commercial telephone service to explain their rights. (In court, immigration judges must repeat the rights advisory. But as one immigration judge said, "Sure, they get the pro bono list and all that, in English or in Spanish . . . which won't help them if they're Punjabi."[70]) The

---

[69] Ibid.

[70] Human Rights Watch interview with an immigration judge who requested anonymity, April 18, 1996.

problem of comprehension is exacerbated by the high illiteracy rates among juvenile detainees; even for Spanish-speaking children, a form in Spanish is no guarantee of comprehension.

Once placed in a county detention facility, children seem to have only sporadic access to telephones. At the Eastlake detention center, Omar, age fifteen, reported that it was difficult to receive incoming calls. This was confirmed by a number of local attorneys; Judy London, who works with CARECEN, an advocacy group for Central American refugees, told us that "it generally takes the Eastlake staff ten phone calls to track down a kid when I show up to visit, and when I tried to call in myself, I was told there was no way to call my client. Finally they said, 'Well, you could try. . .' I said, 'Well, can he call me?' And they said that they weren't sure."[71]

At Los Padrinos, the situation appeared to be worse. INS detainees are kept in a unit with one pay telephone, but the phone was broken at the time of our visit, and the children reported that it had been broken since their arrival. Even had it been working, it was inadequate because it offered no privacy; the pay phone was a wall unit with no surrounding booth, and it was on the wall next to the guard office and in the small lobby containing books and the television set.

> We get access to a phone sometimes every other day . . . but phone use is withheld as a privilege. I'm not sure if I can receive calls. I want to call my relatives in Acapulco but I have no money, and they can't take a collect call because there is only a pay phone in the village.
> —Maria, fifteen[72]

> I don't know my lawyer's telephone number. My husband is in San Pedro [the detention facility for adults], but I can't call him because San Pedro does not take collect calls and I have no money. We have to get permission to make a telephone call.
> —Lorena, seventeen

---

[71] Human Rights Watch interview with Judy London, CARECEN, April 22, 1996.

[72] Human Rights Watch interviews conducted with children at Los Padrinos, April 23, 1996.

> The only call I ever made to my family in Acapulco was in
> December. . . . I asked to make other calls . . . we have to ask
> permission.
> —Rosalia, fifteen, interviewed in April

During our visit to Los Angeles, no Chinese children were in detention, but attorneys told us that in the past, their Chinese clients have encountered even more serious difficulties with telephone calls, because of language problems. Negotiating for permission to use the telephone is difficult enough, but for Chinese speakers, collect calls are nearly impossible. "Some of these kids have never used a phone before," said Gilbert Fung, an attorney who has represented several Chinese children. "They come from tiny villages, and they don't even understand what the different numerals represent. Staff won't help, or they can't, because they don't speak the children's dialect."[73]

Janice Carter, the detention officer in charge of the Los Padrinos unit holding INS children, confirmed that the children are only permitted to make collect calls.[74] This makes it almost impossible for many children to contact their relatives: adult relatives who are themselves detained in INS facilities are unable to accept collect calls, and relatives in the children's home countries often have no private telephones and must rely on a pay telephone in a nearby town. Jan Aven, one of the directors of the Los Padrinos facility, told us that if the pay phone was broken, the children could "use the phone [in the office] whenever they want," but that they can't make calls to numbers outside of the country.[75]

With regard to incoming calls, Ms. Aven first told us, "The policy is to put incoming calls through" to detainees, but she later contradicted this, saying, "We generally don't allow phone calls to come in to the kids, because we can't monitor them, to know who they're really from or what's being discussed. It's a matter of discretion. It's very rare to let calls in . . . . I just take messages. At one point we got some calls when we had a lot of Chinese kids here, and the calls seemed to be pranks. So I stopped putting through calls from people claiming to be calling from

---

[73] Human Rights Watch interview with Gilbert Fung, private immigration attorney, April 20, 1996.

[74] Human Rights Watch interview with Janice Carter, Los Padrinos Juvenile Hall, April 23, 1996.

[75] Human Rights Watch interview with Jan Aven, Director, Los Padrinos Juvenile Hall, April 23, 1996.

China."[76] In other words, staff at Los Padrinos, fearing that *some* calls may be prank calls, no longer permit *any,* where the caller claims to be calling from China.

Even when attorneys and detained children arrange to meet in person, conditions are inadequate. All of the local attorneys reported that they found it difficult to conduct confidential conversations with their clients, since in addition to their practice of monitoring telephone calls, officials at neither Eastlake nor Los Padrinos had an area set aside for private meetings between the children and their attorneys. We confirmed this on our visits. At both Eastlake and Los Padrinos, staff appeared surprised when we asked for a private place to interview children. At Eastlake, we were permitted to interview children outside, sitting at picnic tables, with guards, other children and an INS official standing nearby. At several points during our interviews we had to repeat our request that guards and INS officials remain out of earshot. At Los Padrinos, we interviewed children in their dormitory, which meant that at any given time, the children not being interviewed had to remain outside. Guards and INS officials sat immediately outside of the dorm room, watching us through the windows. In a few cases, those we interviewed were noticeably unsettled by the presence of nearby guards or officials.

The children's inability to receive incoming calls reliably, combined with the difficulty in telephoning relatives outside the country or in INS detention centers elsewhere, the restrictions on telephone usage, and the absence of fully private interview areas for meetings with attorneys, severely interfere with the children's right to contact their legal representatives, to obtain information relevant to their status, and to consult with adult family members.

If children in INS detention find it difficult to locate attorneys and family members, attorneys find it equally difficult to locate current and prospective clients. The INS routinely transfers children from detention facility to detention facility, rarely giving the children, their families or their lawyers notice of the transfers.[77] Almost every child we interviewed in Los Angeles had spent time in more than one county facility; none of the children seemed to understand the reasons, if any, for their transfers.

---

[76] Ibid.

[77] According to the United Nations' High Commissioner for Refugees, "In order to ensure continuity of care and bearing in mind the best interests of the child, changes in residence for unaccompanied children should be limited to a minimum." U.N.H.C.R Note on Policies and Procedures in dealing with Unaccompanied Children Seeking Asylum, Section 7.2.

Los Angeles attorneys and child advocates consistently reported difficulties in locating their clients: "The only way we find out where they're keeping kids is by accident,"said Carlos Holguin, an attorney with the Center for Human and Constitutional Rights.[78] "You start kicking up a fuss about conditions for kids in one spot, the INS just moves them to another. You complain about [Los Padrinos] and they move the kids to Arizona. You complain about Arizona and they transfer them to Texas." Others voiced similar frustrations:

> We started complaining about conditions in Los Angeles . . . so they shipped the kids out for parts unknown, which isn't what we had in mind.
> —Sharon Lowe, County Probation Board[79]

> Usually I get a panicky call, not from the kids, but from a relative, saying, 'My kid is held somewhere in L.A.' So I make twenty calls over two days. Eventually I figure out where the kid is, if I have the name, but it's hard. And if you just want to find out, in general, how many kids are where, it's impossible. We're filing a class action suit about detention conditions, and [the INS] is now under court order to reveal names and locations of class members. We'll see if they do it. Usually the problem is, you never get this information, you just can't get anyone to tell you where the kids are. . . .
> —Judy London, CARECEN[80]

> Sometimes the INS is holding minors but they won't tell you. They throw roadblocks in your way . . . . Sometimes I think the assistant district director doesn't even know where the kids are.

---

[78] Human Rights Watch interview with Carlos Holguin, Center for Human and Constitutional Rights, April 19, 1996.

[79] Human Rights Watch interview with Sharon Lowe, Los Angeles County Probation Board, April 19, 1996.

[80] Human Rights Watch interview with Judy London, CARECEN, April 22, 1996.

—Heidi Sanchez, social worker at Juvenes, an agency that
assists Latin American young people[81]

Without exception, none of the attorneys or other service providers we
met in Los Angeles had been informed by the INS of the decision to transfer most
long-term detainees to the new shelter-care facility in Arizona. "That's news to
me," said Neils Franzen of Public Counsel, Los Angeles's primary multi-issue
non-profit legal aid office. "But it's typical. No one knows what's going on with
the kids. They don't tell us."[82]

In some cases, the INS transferred children out of Los Angeles even after
expressly assuring attorneys that their clients would not be moved. For example,
Gilbert Fung told us that his client had a hearing date set for late May, in Los
Angeles. After hearing a rumor that some children might be transferred to Arizona,
he called David Tally, the detention and deportation officer for the Western Region
of the INS. Tally assured him that his client would remain in Los Angeles. Fung
drove to Los Padrinos to prepare his client for the hearing but was unable to find
the child. He was also unable to find any officials able to tell him where the child
had been moved.

Shortly thereafter, he received an anxious call from his client's family,
who said that they had been unable to contact the child, and that the INS would not
tell them where he was. Fung called David Tally once more and was assured that
only minors with final deportation orders were being transferred to Arizona. That
night, however, the client's relatives called to tell Fung that they had heard from
the child, who gave them a number with an Arizona area code. Fung called Tally
for a third time to report that his client had called his family from Arizona. Tally
said he didn't know why. Fung tried to contact his client at the Arizona facility,
but for two weeks he received no response to his repeated telephone messages. He
eventually confirmed that his client was in Arizona only when the INS filed a
motion for change of venue, in an attempt to move his client's hearing to Arizona.[83]

This raises a related problem. Since the INS began to transfer many
children from Los Angeles to Arizona, the INS has been routinely filing for

---

[81] Human Rights Watch interview with Heidi Sanchez, Juvenes, April 23, 1996.

[82] Human Rights Watch interview with Neils Franzen, Public Counsel, April 23, 1996.

[83] Human Rights Watch interview with Gilbert Fung, private immigration attorney, April 20, 1996.

changes of venue in the case of all transferred children. The INS files for change of venue regardless of whether or not a given child is represented by a Los Angeles-based attorney. Of the children who have legal representation, many are represented pro bono (i.e., for free) by private practitioners or by public interest attorneys, who can ill afford numerous trips to Arizona to meet with clients and attend court hearings. Even in the case of children with relatives able to hire private attorneys, changes of venue, if successful, add greatly to the costs of representation, since either the child or the attorney must travel long distances for consultations. The INS blanket policy of requesting changes of venue seriously interferes with the children's right to effective assistance of counsel.[84]

But for children detained in Los Angeles, having an attorney is a luxury. In all of Los Angeles, only about half a dozen attorneys will represent indigent juvenile detainees, and with high caseloads, drastic funding cuts, and restrictions on Legal Resources Corporation recipients, that number is dwindling. "Everyone's case load is just too high," said Lorena Muñoz, a Legal Aid lawyer. "These kids slip between the cracks."[85] At CARECEN, budget cuts mean that there is no one to staff the switchboard. "We're on the legal services list the kids get," said CARECEN's Judy London. "So maybe they call us. But no one will answer. They have to leave a message . . . and I just can't take all the cases." At Public Counsel, Neils Franzen was blunt: "It's uncommon for kids to get represented."[86]

One immigration judge who spoke to us off the record confirmed this. "Kids under sixteen can't admit deportability without a lawyer or a responsible adult present . . . . I take this seriously, and I get on the phone, trying to make sure those kids get lawyers. But all the INS people in Washington care about are the numbers, so we're under a lot of pressure just to move things along faster . . . That's a problem for kids, who can't get counsel. There are ways to get around the

---

[84] The change of venue policy was defended, in our view inadequately, on the grounds that it was a "child welfare measure." John Salter, Los Angeles INS District Counsel, asserted that the INS files C.O.V.'s "To save the child the hardship of traveling. Why should the child have to come all the way back all that way for hearings, and be on all that transportation and everything? It's too hard on them." Human Rights Watch interview with John Salter, April 23, 1996.

[85] Human Rights Watch interview with Lorena Muñoz, Legal Aid Foundation of Los Angeles, April 22, 1996.

[86] Human Rights Watch interview with Niels Franzen, Public Counsel, April 23, 1996.

rules, and it's in the judge's discretion to decide who's a 'responsible person.' In other judges' courtrooms, I just don't know what happens to these kids. There aren't enough lawyers for them . . . The kids are scared . . . . Generally they don't know what the hell is going on."[87]

This comment sums up the situation for most children in INS detention, both in Los Angeles and in Arizona. Over and over, the children we met told us that they did not understand their legal situation:

> They told me I'd be deported on December 30, but I'm still here [in late April]. I haven't heard anything since then. No one from the INS has talked to me since December 15. I don't know what is happening.
> —Jaime, fifteen

> I think I will be deported . . . . I don't know what's up, I don't want to fight anymore . . . I just don't know what's up, you know?
> —Jorge, seventeen

> I don't know why I am here for so long. No one explains why they won't let me go. I heard someone say, if they let me go, I would go back to Mexico.
> —Maria, fifteen

> I don't know what is going on with my case. No one has contacted me since November. [We spoke to Mercedes in April.] When I ask people here, they say, 'Well, there's no news, when they want you they'll come and get you.
> —Mercedes, seventeen

> I don't know why we are staying here, I don't know anything about my case, I don't care if it's over . . . I just want to get out of here and go home.
> —Ana, fifteen

---

[87] Human Rights Watch interview with immigration judge who requested anonymity, April 18, 1996.

> When I ask the guards what is happening, they just say, 'Be
> patient. . .'
> —Jose, eighteen

Arizona

> Many kids want to call their relatives but they are not allowed.
> They are sad and they cry.
> —Shiao-yun, seventeen

In late March 1996, the INS began to transfer most longer-term juvenile detainees to a new "shelter-care" facility in Arizona.[88] The facility is run (under contract to the INS) by a private Texas-based company called Southwest Key, which specializes in running juvenile detention centers. The facility was created specifically to satisfy the *Flores* requirements and to implement improvements over conditions in Los Angeles County detention facilities. In their operation of the facility, Southwest Key is legally required to comply with detailed guidelines, distributed by the Department of Justice, concerning all aspects of the children's care and rights.[89]

To date, however, there is overwhelming evidence that children detained at the Arizona facility are also being denied their right to legal information and representation. In many ways, the culpability of the INS and its agents in Arizona is even greater than in Los Angeles: in Los Angeles, children suffer primarily because they slip between the cracks, and many of the INS officials to whom we spoke seemed largely unaware of conditions for children. But if problems in Los Angeles stemmed largely from INS ignorance, incompetence and indifference, the problems in Arizona appear to exist with the deliberate and active cooperation of INS and Southwest Key officials.

The Arizona facility has space for forty-eight children. As in Los Angeles, we were unable to obtain long-term statistics on children passing through the Arizona facility. Although we were provided with information on the age, nationality and gender of children in detention at the time of our site visit, we were not able to obtain statistics on the ultimate disposition of children passing through

---

[88] We were allowed to visit the Arizona facility only on condition that we not reveal its precise location.

[89] Alien Minors Shelter Care Program, Program Guidelines and Requirements, U.S. Department of Justice, Community Relations Service. No date is available for this document.

the facility. No one at the facility or the Phoenix district INS office was willing to reveal whether such statistics exist. However, it appears from interviews with children and local attorneys that one half to three-fourths of the children are Chinese, and that many children remain in the facility for months at a time.

The facility is in a remote town, roughly an hour and a half from Tucson and an hour from Phoenix. Unlike Los Angeles, in which detained children are at least in geographical proximity to community groups and legal service providers, the Arizona facility is far from any sizable city, and far from a substantial community of service providers. In Phoenix, there is no provider of free legal services to undocumented children, and in Tucson, only one group—the Tucson Ecumenical Council Legal Assistance (TECLA)—provides legal services to indigent children. TECLA, however, is able to serve only Spanish-speaking children, leaving non-Spanish-speaking children, including the many Chinese children, with no means of obtaining free legal assistance. Some of the children in the Arizona facility are sent there straight from being detained at the airport, but many come after spending days or weeks in detention in Los Angeles.

At the Arizona facility, we were permitted to interview the children only for ten minutes each (fifteen minutes for Chinese children, with whom we required an interpreter), making it difficult to accurately assess each child's situation. The Phoenix district of the INS also required us, before speaking to the children, to sign an affidavit promising not to discuss the specifics of any child's legal situation with that child. However, even these brief interviews made it overwhelmingly clear that children in the Arizona facility are being denied access to the most essential (and legally required) information.[90] Of the fifteen children we interviewed, over half reported that they had never received a list containing information about legal services. Many of the children knew that such a list existed, and that a few children had copies, but said that staff at the facility failed to give the lists to all children. Copies of the list were not posted anywhere in the facility.

---

[90] Facility staff must provide minors with "information regarding the availability of free legal assistance. . . . the right to be represented by counsel at no expense to the government . . . the right to a deportation or exclusion hearing before an immigration judge. . . [and] that they may apply for political asylum or request voluntary departure in lieu of deportation." Staff at facilities "shall assist minors in making confidential contact with attorneys and their authorized representatives. An accurate and current reference list of voluntary agencies and attorneys who provide services without compensation will be posted and provided to all minors." Alien Minors Shelter Care Program, Program Guidelines and Requirements, U.S. Department of Justice, Community Relations Service.

"They told me that, since I wasn't going to be deported, since I was going to be reunited with my family, I didn't need the list," said Ernesto, a sixteen-year-old Salvadoran. Vilma, fifteen, reported that although a teacher did distribute a list in class, "I went out [and] when I came back it was gone . . . nobody has it now . . . I want to get an attorney." Huang Li, seventeen, could not recall ever seeing the list. Nien He, seventeen, had been at the facility for ten days but had not received the list, had not been to court, had not seen an attorney, and, during the interview, said that he did not know what an attorney was. Chi-Ping, seventeen, said that she did not know how to contact a lawyer, and that staff had told her that she could find a lawyer after she got out of the facility. Again and again, the children reported that they had not seen a list of legal service providers, and that staff, when asked for information about lawyers, told the children that they would not need a lawyer. One of the teachers at the facility reportedly told an entire classroom of children that they did not need copies of the list.

The INS requires contracting shelter-care facilities to assist children in reuniting with family members living in the United States.[91] Family reunification, ideally, serves a two-fold purpose: first, it is preferable for humanitarian reasons to release children to family members instead of detaining them for an indefinite period, and second, detention is at government expense, and releasing children to family members relieves the government of that economic burden. It appears, however, that staff at the Arizona facility use the laudable goal of family reunification for an illegitimate purpose: that of preventing children from getting legal representation. Children repeatedly informed us that staff members had told them that they did not need a lawyer if they were going to be reunited with their families before their deportation hearings. But, as long as they are in detention, the children's right to representation is unaffected by whether or not they will ultimately be released to family members pending deportation hearings. Detained children require counsel not only to assist them in deportation proceedings but also to enable them to challenge detention conditions, if necessary. Finally, since children released to family members must nonetheless go through deportation proceedings, preventing children from getting a lawyer at the earliest possible opportunity may merely cause significant and sometimes damaging delays in the legal process.

Even those children who do receive the legal services list are handicapped, because the list contains inaccurate and incomplete information. Of the free legal service providers whose numbers appear on the list, several receive federal Legal

---

[91] Department of Justice, Alien Minors Shelter Care Program, Program Guidelines and Requirements.

Services Corporation funds and therefore are prohibited from representing undocumented children. Of the rest, only TECLA routinely assists undocumented indigent children. None of the legal services providers listed have Chinese-speaking capabilities, although when we visited the Arizona facility, more than half of the children detained there spoke only Chinese.

One of the Chinese-speaking staff members at the facility allegedly referred several children who wanted legal assistance to a relative of his in Pennsylvania, who reportedly charged a minimum of $2,500 to represent each child.[92] Several children also told attorneys that facility staff became less friendly to them once they discovered that the child had successfully obtained outside legal representation.

Children at the Arizona facility also lack meaningful access to telephones. During the first two weeks of its operation, the facility had no telephone; as far as their Los Angeles-based attorneys and their families were concerned, children taken to Arizona had vanished off the face of the earth. There are still no private pay telephones available for the children's use. Instead, children must use telephones in staff offices, with no assurance of privacy. One attorney told us that, on repeated occasions, telephone calls to clients were monitored by Southwest Key staff.

Staff at the facility assured us that children have unrestricted private access to phones for purposes of obtaining representation and contacting family members,[93] but this was contradicted by local attorneys and by the children we interviewed. Gloria Goldman, the attorney appointed by a local immigration judge to find pro bono representation for children at hearings, reported that children

---

[92] This practice, a clear conflict of interest, was investigated by the Office of the Inspector General of the Department of Justice. The complaint that sparked the investigation originated from someone outside the Southwest Key facility. (Whether Southwest Key staff knew of this practice and permitted it to continue is unclear.) The OIG investigation, initiated in August 1996 and closed in January 1997, found no evidence of criminal conduct, but did confirm that the staff member in question had contacted people outside of the facility and engaged in activities "outside the realm of his work." Human Rights Watch interview with Bill King, Special Agent in Charge, Tucson OIG, January 7, 1997. The OIG also confirmed that the staff member in question had been suspended by Southwest Key soon after the OIG investigation began, and had not returned to seek reinstatement as of January 1997.

[93] Human Rights Watch interview with Melissa Jenkins, director of Arizona facility, May 21, 1996.

appeared able to use the telephones only every other week.[94] Patsy Kraeger, the chair of the Arizona Immigration Law Association, reported that she met with one child who had been at the facility for two months without being able to contact his family, because his telephone access was so limited. She offered him the use of her cellular phone, and he was able to reach his family right away.[95] Kraeger also recalls a child who told her that phone use was reserved as a privilege for children who got "stars" for good behavior. Several children told our researcher this as well.

The children we interviewed spoke constantly of the difficulty in contacting anyone by telephone. Children reported that they were not permitted to receive incoming calls from family members outside the Unites States, and many children were upset at their inability to contact adult family members held by the INS at the adult detention center in Florence, Arizona—since neither facility will accept collect calls, the children have no way of calling relatives or receiving calls from them.[96] Children must ask for permission to use the telephone, and permission is routinely and arbitrarily refused.

Shiao-Yun, seventeen, reported that the staff do not let her call her uncle, although he has called her. Staff repeatedly tell children that if their relatives want to talk to them, "They'll call you, you don't need to call them." According to Shiao-yun, "Many kids want to call their relatives but they are not allowed . . . they are sad and they cry." Iwei, seventeen, said that "You have to apply to make a phone call—it's difficult. They always ask why you want to call . . . you have to answer." Yung-Chi, seventeen, also reported being told that he had to apply to make telephone calls, "but that is difficult to do." Ming-Yang, sixteen, said that she had not yet called her relatives in her two weeks at the facility. When she asked to make a call, she was told that there was no need, and that her relatives would call her.

Che-Hao, sixteen, asked for permission to call his cousin to congratulate her on getting married. He wrote a note asking for permission to call her, but permission was denied. He was permitted to call relatives in China in order to get

---

[94] Human Rights Watch interview with Gloria Goldman, immigration attorney, May 23, 1996.

[95] Human Rights Watch interview with Patsy Kraeger, Chair, Arizona Immigration Law Association, June 7, 1996.

[96] This highlights a related problem: the lack of INS detention facilities for families.

numbers of relatives in the U.S., "but I am only allowed to say two sentences: where I am, and what is the phone number of a relative. These were calls to my mother, and I was only allowed to say two sentences, then the staff hung up the phone." Sung Bae, sixteen, said that it is "very difficult" to make a call, and he does not understand why. When he asks to call, staff normally say no. He is permitted to contact a cousin every few weeks. Esteban, sixteen, reported, "When you ask to make a call, [staff] say they're going to make it [for you], but they don't. This happens to everyone."

As with the Los Angeles County facilities, Arizona lawyers have experienced difficulties in gaining access to children. The only organization in the region that provides legal assistance to indigent undocumented children is TECLA, but TECLA lawyers told us that they have consistently found facility staff and INS officials uncooperative and hostile. TECLA attorney Deirdre Mokos approached the INS to get names of children in the facility who required legal assistance, but the INS refused to provide her with the names of children. Mokos also told us that when she visited the facility to interview clients, staff members intruded into confidential discussions with clients, and her telephone conversations with clients were also monitored by staff.[97]

The INS and the facility staff initially permitted Deirdre Mokos to visit the facility and give presentations to the children on their legal rights, but after Mokos began to express her concern that many children were unrepresented, the staff refused to permit her to continue making presentations. A variety of explanations were given for the refusal to permit the rights presentations; Mokos was sometimes told that the dates and times were inconvenient, and she was also informed that the presentations were unnecessary because all of the children were represented, and that several Phoenix non-profits were representing the children. When we spoke to representatives of the non-profits mentioned, however, they said that they had no contact with the facility or the children. TECLA has been unable to visit the facility to give rights presentations since April 25, 1996.[98]

Representatives of the INS and the Southwest Key facility assured Human Rights Watch that all children were represented by attorneys, but they refused to give out the names of the attorneys. Interviews with the children, however, made it clear that many—if not most—of the children were unrepresented. Deirdre Mokos of TECLA was also informed that all children were represented, and did

---

[97] Human Rights Watch interview with Deirdre Mokos, Tucson Ecumenical Council Legal Assistance (TECLA), May 15 and June 7, 1996.

[98] Human Rights Watch interview with Deirdre Mokos, May 15, 1996.

receive some names of attorneys, but when she called the attorneys, hoping to discuss ways of coordinating their efforts, they told her that they were not representing any children. Not only did the INS and facility staff significantly misrepresent the extent to which detained children are represented, but they made it overwhelmingly difficult for children to obtain representation on their own initiative.

In mid-1996, a local immigration judge initiated a program whereby children are represented at their initial calender hearings by attorneys working pro bono. This representation, though, is largely a matter of legal fiction. As discussed in the legal background section of this report, immigration judges are prohibited from accepting admissions of deportability made by unrepresented children under sixteen. If a child is unrepresented, the judge must either continue the case until the child acquires a representative or hold a merit hearing on the issue, in which the INS would bear the burden of proving that the child is deportable. In either case, this would substantially delay the deportation process.[99] In an effort to expedite the process, Immigration Judge John Richardson asked area attorneys to volunteer their services for the children's initial calendar hearings (at which they admit deportability, declare a defense to deportability, or seek a continuance).[100]

Not surprisingly, local attorneys who have volunteered to represent children on calendar days have mixed feelings about their role. Gloria Goldman, who was asked to coordinate the pro bono effort, says that most attorneys will only have an hour to meet the children before their hearing; with a full docket, this gives attorneys six minutes per child. Similarly, Jennifer Huang, a Tucson attorney, told us that she was assured that her commitment was only for one day's calendar, and

---

[99] In a deportation hearing, the INS, as the prosecution, bears the burden of proving that a given child is deportable. The simplest way for the INS to prove this is by obtaining a straightforward admission of deportability from a child, or, failing that, by getting a child to make damaging and contradictory statements while testifying. But since the regulations prohibit immigration judges from accepting admissions of deportability from children under 16 who are not accompanied by a lawyer or adult friend or relative, any damaging admissions made by such a child will not be admissible as evidence. In the case of such children, the INS must resort to proving deportability through evidence other than the child's own testimony (for instance, INS lawyers might have to introduce expert testimony about conditions in the child's home country or region). This can lead to a more drawn out and costly process.

[100] Judge Richardson did not return a call to Human Rights Watch, but various attorneys described this program to us, including INS Phoenix District Counsel Pat Vroom, in a telephone interview on November 13, 1996.

that if any of the children refused to admit deportability, but instead applied for asylum, she could withdraw from the representation. She said that she had represented approximately ten children at each calendar date, with about two hours to meet and interview them before going into court.[101] This works out to roughly ten minutes per child, clearly an inadequate amount of time, especially since some attorneys need interpreters. Goldman candidly expressed her apprehension about the program she coordinates, saying, "I don't want to be a vehicle for kids to be deported."[102]

In a November 1996 telephone interview with Human Rights Watch, INS Phoenix District Counsel Pat Vroom expressed her frustration that TECLA continued to seek access to detained children for the purpose of giving legal rights presentations and assuring dissemination of required legal information. "All of these kids are represented!" she insisted. On inquiry, we learned that she was referring to the pro bono representation at calendar hearings. Our researcher asked, "Don't you think it's a stretch to say that these kids are represented, when they don't know they have an attorney, have never seen or spoken to an attorney, and will not meet an attorney until shortly before their hearing?" Reluctantly, District Counsel Vroom agreed that to say these children are represented is indeed "a stretch."[103]

District Counsel Vroom also acknowledged that "there are a few problems" with the current pro bono calendar hearing arrangement. "The system is not perfect yet," she said. "Some attorneys are getting saddled with lots of work, while others just stand there and get cases continued until the following date—this creates some confusion as to who [which attorney] is to handle the cases."[104]

Surprisingly, given her position as district counsel, Ms. Vroom also told Human Rights Watch that she was largely uninformed about the legal situation of the detained children. "This has all been very fluid," she said. "I don't know

---

[101] Interview with Jennifer Huang, immigration attorney, May 20, 1996.

[102] Human Rights Watch interview with Gloria Goldman, immigration attorney, May 20, 1996.

[103] Human Its Watch interview with INS Phoenix District Counsel Pat Vroom, November 13, 1996.

[104] Ibid.

exactly what's going on with the handling of legal cases."[105] Nor, despite more than seven months of disagreements with TECLA over the suspended legal rights presentations (last permitted by the INS in April 1996), had she inquired into the possibility of having routine presentations done by a different organization, by a law school clinic, or by rotating members of the immigration bar, to name just a few possibilities.[106]

---

[105] Ibid.

[106] Mrs. Vroom also admitted that she and her staff had not contacted other shelter-care facilities or other INS districts to see how they ensured protection of detainees' legal rights, including the right to receive legal information and the right to assistance in obtaining legal representation of one's choosing.

IV. CONDITIONS OF CONFINEMENT

Every day is a kind of punishment, to be imprisoned here.
—Jorge, seventeen, detained at the Arizona facility

Everything is very sad and bleak here.
—Josefina, seventeen, detained at Los Padrinos

In 1985, the extremely poor conditions of confinement in Los Angeles facilities gave rise to the *Flores* lawsuit and the subsequent consent decree, discussed earlier in this report. Los Angeles lawyers who represent unaccompanied children report that immediately after the settlement, conditions in county facilities did improve somewhat, but that they soon deteriorated again. The plaintiffs in the *Flores* class action suit have returned to California district court in an effort to enforce the terms of the settlement decree, and are now in the process of negotiating a second settlement with the INS. Unfortunately, given the absence of monitoring and oversight and the inability of most children to obtain adequate representation, it seems unlikely that the new settlement will have any more effect that the first. This is particularly likely to be the case given that conditions in Arizona—in a facility designed specifically to meet the already-stringent *Flores* requirements—are also poor.

Los Angeles County

Children detained in Los Angeles county are normally sent to county facilities for juvenile offenders, even though children in INS detention are being detained for administrative reasons only. The INS currently claims that all children who do not pose a "security risk" will be sent to Arizona, and that only children with some history of contact with the criminal justice system will be held in Los Angeles. Most of the children we interviewed in Los Angeles were children who had initially been picked up by police and charged with misdemeanors before being turned over to the INS. All of these children were, however, being detained only because of their immigration status, and not because of any pending criminal sentences or delinquency dispositions.

We also interviewed three young girls being held as material witnesses against Mexican smuggling gangs. The girls were brought into the United States by a gang of smugglers, and when police raided the smugglers' house, the girls, though charged with no crime, were detained for immigration reasons. Since they were also potential witnesses in the government's case against the smugglers, they were eventually transferred by the INS to the legal custody of the U.S. Marshals. When the cases for which they are witnesses are over, they will again revert to the legal custody of the INS. (The INS acting assistant district director called them "once and future INS detainees.")[107] Staff at the county facility holding them seemed unsure of whether the children were under the control of the INS or the Marshals, and the girls themselves had no idea. At the time we interviewed them, the girls had been in detention for over a year.

The INS is unwilling to guarantee that county detention centers will not in the future be used again even for children who pose no security risk, if space is unavailable elsewhere.[108] Thus, although at the time of our visit fewer than ten INS detainees were at the county facilities, poor conditions remain a matter of urgent concern.

The most fundamental problem with detention facilities in Los Angeles is that they are prisons. For any children who are not security risks, this clearly violates the *Flores* requirements. Given the apparently arbitrary process through which the INS declares some children to be security risks, this violates the rights of many "security risk" children as well. "These children—even the security risks—are supposed to be detained, not incarcerated," said Sharon Lowe, a lawyer and member of the Los Angeles County Probation Board. "But basically they are incarcerated. The INS doesn't call it that, but that's what it is."[109]

Eastlake, Los Padrinos and Sylmar are all surrounded by barbed-wire fences. To reach the units where children are housed, visitors must pass through several guard stations and locked doors. (During our visit, no INS detainees were at Sylmar, and the INS says that they plan to stop using Sylmar). At both Eastlake and Los Padrinos, INS detainees are forbidden to wear their own clothes and must instead wear white or orange prison uniforms, many of them stamped with the words "Detention Bureau" on the legs and sleeves.

At Eastlake, boys in INS detention were housed in a dormitory-like setting; each bedroom contained anywhere from two to six or eight beds. Girls, both INS detainees and adjudicated offenders, were housed together in one enormous barracks-like room containing about forty beds; neither boys nor girls had access to private toilet facilities. Toilets were at the side of each room, but

---

[107] Human Rights Watch interview with Leonard Kovensky, acting deputy district director of the INS, Los Angeles District, April 18, 1996.

[108] Human Rights Watch interview with Rosemary Melville, Acting District Director of the INS, Los Angeles District, April 25, 1996.

[109] Human Rights Watch interview with Sharon Lowe, Los Angeles County Probation Board, April 19, 1996.

neither toilets nor shower stalls had doors. When we visited the boys' unit at Eastlake, the boys were all marched in together after their recreation period and made to strip down to their underpants in a large room, separated from observers of both sexes only by large glass windows.

At Los Padrinos, boys and girls in INS detention are housed in the same small unit, which has room for only sixteen children. Boys (none were there during our visit) occupied one room off the central corridor, with girls in a room off the other side of the corridor. Each room was about twenty feet by twenty feet, and had a row of small windows facing the courtyard. The windows could not be opened, however, and were painted black on their lower halves, so that only the sky could be seen through the top half of the windows. Each room contained eight metal cots, each with a thin blanket. Each room also contained one toilet, a sink and a shower cubicle, none of which had doors. The cinder block walls were entirely bare. Each child had a small locker in which to keep personal possessions, but the children were not permitted to display personal possessions around their beds. Of the three girls we met at Los Padrinos, two (both material witnesses) had been there for over a year without ever leaving the facility, except for court dates.

> I don't like this place. The food is bad, the clothes they make us wear are ugly and they don't fit. At night it gets cold. I have never left this place in a year. We can keep school books in the lockers, but they do not lock . . . we are not allowed to put up pictures . . . some of the staff are nice, some are not. When they have personal problems they take them out on us. We can have books, but the books are all in English, and the television is in English. We can go out and play [in the courtyard in front of the unit], but you have to have [a staff member] go with you. You can't go out alone. There is nowhere here to be alone. If you are bad—if you do not do your exercise, or use bad language—they send you to "the box."[110] Then you are alone in a room, with nothing.
> —Marielena, fifteen

---

[110] Staff members described "the box" as a medical isolation chamber to which kids were occasionally sent when they posed a behavioral problem. It is a small windowless room containing a metal cot, a sink and a toilet. International human rights standards forbid the use of solitary confinement for children. U.N. Rules for the Protection of Juveniles Deprived of their Liberty, Rule 67.

> Everything is very sad and bleak here. They take all of your
> property and your clothes when you come in. You can only go
> out of the room with staff, and if you do not do your exercise,
> you get in trouble, you go to the box. The TV is in English, and
> there is no radio. Sometimes there are more kids here, and they
> are from different gangs and neighborhoods, and they fight.[111]
> —Josefina, seventeen

All of the children we interviewed said that they were frustrated by their inability to get any privacy and by their difficulty in getting reading materials in their own language. During our visit, there were no non-Spanish-speaking children in the Los Angeles facilities; local attorneys report that non-Spanish-speaking children have an even more difficult time than children from Latin America, who can usually find Spanish-speaking staff members.   Very few of the county detention center staff speak Chinese.

The result, said attorney Gilbert Fung, is that "Chinese kids get herded around like sheep. Staff can't communicate with them, so they basically just push and pull the kids to get them to go somewhere. The education is meaningless for these children—they just sit and listen, but have no idea what's going on. Even the food is a problem—they don't know what American food is. They're used to rice and noodles, and they are given food that's too salty, too rich . . . Most get sick in their first week in detention, but they don't know how to ask for doctors."[112]

Neither the INS nor the facility staff bring in interpreters. This not only means that children have little meaningful access to legal information, but also greatly increases the level of psychological stress for many children, who find themselves arrested and put in jail, all with no way of understanding what is happening to them. As in the B-18 staging area, staff at detention centers rely on the AT&T telephone interpretation service in emergencies. "Sometimes we have a kid who's crying and crying, and we can't figure out what's wrong . . . so we call AT&T and ask the operator to speak to the kid."[113]

---

[111] Human Rights Watch site visit to Los Padrinos, April 23, 1996.

[112] Human Rights Watch interview with Gilbert Fung, immigration attorney, April 20, 1996.

[113] Human Rights Watch interview with Jan Aven, Director, Los Padrinos Juvenile Hall, April 23, 1996.

Although relying on commercial telephone operators to communicate with crying, bewildered children hardly seems like an adequate form of counseling, the alternatives that normally occur to the INS are little better. Lorena Muñoz, a legal aid lawyer, told us about one of her clients: "I had a Pakistani kid who spoke no English, and he was so scared and depressed, he was suicidal. We got an interpreter and we had him observed, and the psychologist said yes, he was suicidal. We told the INS, and so they evaluated him—in English! And they said he was fine."[114]

Children detained in county facilities suffer most from sheer neglect. Put in prison, they receive virtually nothing in the way of counseling, are seldom visited, and leave their units only to go to court hearings. Recreation consists of television, often in a language they do not understand, and mandatory calisthenics. When taken to court, children remain in their prison uniforms, and local attorneys report that the children are regularly transported in shackles. Children are often taken to court at odd hours and made to wait all day in holding cells; as a result, missed meals are frequent. "Kids get brought in at weird hours, like three in the morning. It's just whenever the INS feels like transporting them. So they miss breakfast because they're being transported, and they miss lunch because of the hearing."[115]

Commingling has been an ongoing problem in Los Angeles. Children are sometimes placed in adult detention centers, or kept overnight with unrelated adults in the holding cells at B-18. Local attorneys allege that, on some occasions, children have had to sleep for several nights in offices in the federal building when space in county facilities was unavailable. Even more common is commingling of administrative INS detainees with juvenile offenders currently serving sentences. Virtually every lawyer we spoke to reported finding INS administrative detainees mixed in with the general prison population at one time or another. On our visits, it seemed that children at Los Padrinos were segregated from the general population and mixed only with status offenders; the same appeared to be true of boys at Eastlake. But all the girls at Eastlake were mixed in together, regardless of category.

---

[114] Human Rights Watch interview with Lorena Münoz, Legal Aid Foundation of Los Angeles, April 22, 1996.

[115] Human Rights Watch interview with Judy London, CARECEN, April 22, 1996.

Arizona

The Arizona facility is a nondescript two-story building on a rural road, several miles from the nearest town. The grounds are surrounded by an eight-foot-high fence, and access to the grounds is controlled by a guard. The building itself is also locked, and monitored by electronic surveillance cameras. Inside, the facility consists of two levels. The downstairs level holds offices, classrooms, a meeting room and a recreation room with a ping-pong table, a foosball table and a television. The classrooms are small, and extremely crowded when full. The upper level contains dormitories for the children. There are two rooms for girls, one with seven beds and one with three. The girls' bathroom, in the hall, has three toilet stalls, three sinks and two showers. Boys sleep in one of two large rooms; together, the rooms hold thirty-five beds. Despite the much larger number of boys than girls in the facility, the boys' bathroom is the same size as the girls' bathroom. One boy told us that because of overcrowding, they are hurried through the bathrooms ("We don't fit"); after the girls wash up in the morning, boys are sent in to use their bathroom.

The children normally spend only an hour a day outside, during supervised physical education from 8:00 a.m. to 9:00 a.m. The rest of the time they are indoors, either in class or in other supervised activities. Several children complained that they are never allowed outside for unstructured play. The director of the facility told us that the children's outdoor time is curtailed because the intense desert heat might be harmful to them. But while this explanation implies a laudable concern for the well-being of the children, it was belied by reports we received from the children: while not allowed out to play, they told us that they are sometimes made to work outside as punishment for minor disciplinary infractions. One boy we interviewed told us that he has just come in from four hours outside, cleaning the grounds.[116]

INS policy requires that the children be taken on field trips at least once a week.[117] Staff at the facility told us that they take the children on one field trip every six weeks. While this in itself represents a major violation of INS regulations, the children we interviewed reported even less frequent field trips. During their period of detention at the Southwest Key facility (a period which, for the children we interviewed, ranged from one week to seven months, and averaged two

---

[116] Human Rights Watch interview, Southwest Key facility, June 13, 1996.

[117] U.S. Department of Justice: Alien Minors Shelter Care Program, Program Guidelines and Requirements: "All minors shall be afforded opportunities for escorted visits to the surrounding communities for leisure activities at least twice each week."

months), only three of the fifteen children with whom we spoke had ever been off the premises for a reason other than a court date. Two of these three children—both girls who had been in detention for about two months—were taken to a shopping mall in Phoenix on the day before our site visit. The other child who had been taken on a field trip was a boy, Ernesto, who had also been detained for two months. He reported that he was taken to Phoenix for a day, along with four other boys, and said that "It was like a prize. You had to have sufficient points." Another boy, Yung Chi, told us that "You're allowed to go on a field trip if you have enough points. Most of us have enough points, but [still are not allowed to go out]." At the time of our visit, Yung Chi, like another boy we interviewed, had been in detention for seven months (four months in Los Angeles County facilities and three in Arizona), without ever going on a single field trip.[118]

INS policy also requires that children be given the opportunity to engage in religious worship should they desire to do so.[119] At the INS facility in Arizona, this right is observed in the most cursory fashion. A small and uninviting altar is tucked away in a corner of the lot outside the facility, next to the gravel driveway and the eight-foot metal fence. It offers no protection from the sun, and only a small, cracked concrete bench for children to sit upon. Southwest Key staff told us that children were permitted to go to "the prayer center" in groups of two or three at a time, under staff supervision. There is no arrangement to have clergy visit the facility, nor any provision made for the children to attend services in nearby towns.[120]

None of the children we interviewed were aware of any opportunity to worship, nor were most aware of the existence of the small altar. (The altar is in the front of the building, and the children are only permitted to be on the grounds behind the building). One boy, Nien He, told us that he knew that they were not allowed to play by the altar, but did not know whether or not worship was permitted there: "A staff person showed it to us, and then we never went there

---

[118] Human Rights Watch interviews conducted with children detained at the Southwest Key Facility, June 13, 1996.

[119] U.S. Department of Justice: Alien Minors Shelter Care Program, Program Guidelines and Requirements: "[The] daily routine . . . shall include . . . access to . . . religious services. . . . Whenever possible, minors are to be afforded access to religious services of their choice."

[120] Human Rights Watch interviews with children detained at the Southwest Key facility, June 13, 1996.

again . . . . No one has ever told me that I can worship here [at the facility]." Nien He and several other children, most of them practicing Chinese Christians, told us that they would like opportunities to attend religious services. Another Chinese boy told us, "I am a Christian, but there is no possibility of worshiping here." A third boy reported being told by staff that someone would come from a church to lead services for the children, "But no one ever came . . . I would like to go to church. Here, the only time I can pray is when I go to bed at night."[121]

Although INS policy requires that children be given access to public libraries,[122] none of the children had ever been to the library, and none seemed aware of the possibility of going to libraries. Staff did not appear to be offering children these opportunities. The facility itself has no library, and children reported difficulties in getting reading material: "There are no books or magazines to read. The only reading we do is in class," said Villa, age fifteen. Li Zhen, seventeen, said that there were some books and magazines, but reading them was only allowed in class.

The facility is operated with a breathtaking level of cultural insensitivity. Mauricio, seventeen, told us that sometimes, as punishment, the Spanish-speaking children are made to sit in class or attend meals with the Chinese children. Li Zhen told us that staff told all the Chinese children "to behave like Americans, not like Chinese. They tell us to act like good Americans, not like bad Chinese." Several Chinese children complained about the food; Cheng Sha, seventeen, told us that the facility only serves Chinese food when visitors come.[123]

In theory, good behavior will earn children extra privileges, while bad behavior results in the denial of privileges. INS policy requires facilities to provide students with a written explanation of facility rules, in a language they can understand. None of the children we met appeared to understand on what basis, if any, privileges were granted or withdrawn. One Chinese girl recalled getting a card in English, explaining the point system, but said she could not read it and no one explained it to her. Several children told us that although they had many points, they still did not get the privileges to which they were ostensibly entitled. Almost all of the children also complained about the lack of privacy. Children are not

---

[121] Ibid.

[122] U.S. Department of Justice: Alien Minors Shelter Care Program, Program Guidelines and Requirements.

[123] Human Rights Watch interviews conducted with children detained at the Southwest Key Facility, June 13, 1996.

permitted to remain alone in their rooms, reading or thinking; they are always together and always supervised. In general, one boy told us, "Every day is a kind of punishment, to be imprisoned here. . . ."[124]

---

[124] Ibid.

V. THE ROLE OF THE INS

During our mission, we were able to speak to fewer than thirty children, and we had to conduct interviews in highly unsatisfactory conditions. We were only able to speak to each child for a short time. In Los Angeles we had to speak to children in semi-public settings, and in Arizona we were not allowed to speak to children about any aspect of their legal cases, nor for more than ten minutes per child. (Normally, a Human Rights Watch interview with a detained child would be for thirty to forty-five minutes.) The INS told us that they do not keep comprehensive statistics on children in its custody, and we were therefore unable to obtain precise information about the number of children ultimately deported, the number who successfully filed asylum claims, or the number who were released at some point to family members living in the United States.[125] The information we obtained was thus incomplete and anecdotal, but our findings accord with the observations of many public interest lawyers who represent detained children, as well as with affidavits submitted by children in pending court cases. Our findings also accord in broad outline with the findings of researchers with Physicians for Human Rights, who interviewed juvenile INS detainees in Texas and Michigan.[126] We therefore believe that our findings can be generalized, and point to a pattern of ongoing violations of the rights of children in INS detention.

Children in INS detention are systematically denied rights that are fundamental under international agreements and under the U.S. Constitution and statutory law: they are denied due process, denied access to legal representation,

---

[125] In the 1993 Supreme Court Case *Flores v. Reno*, the INS supplied the court with some estimates on the number of unaccompanied children apprehended annually. *Flores v. Reno*, 113 S.Ct. 1439,1443 (1993)(Quoting INS briefs). But when we requested similar statistics for more recent years, Elizabeth Herskovitz, an INS detention and deportation officer in Washington, D.C., explained that the INS does not track dispositions in juvenile cases: "I don't know how they would have gotten those statistics in *Flores v. Reno*. In our statistics, we don't separately track juveniles and adults. It would present tremendous data-gathering problems, and we have never had a reason to keep those statistics. To us, a deportation is a deportation, whether it is an adult or a juvenile. Also, where would you stop, once you start breaking the statistics into categories? Someone might say, you should keep statistics on how many senior citizens get deported." Human Rights Watch interview with Elizabeth Herskovitz, INS detention and deportation officer, December 11, 1996.

[126] Physicians for Human Rights, "Unaccompanied Children in Detention in the U.S.: At Risk for Abuse and Neglect," unpublished report, 1995.

denied humane living conditions, denied personal privacy, and denied meaningful opportunities to understand what is happening to them and why. If they wish to remain in the United States, they must negotiate their way through a maze of technical and bewilderingly complex legal procedures, all in a language and setting utterly foreign to them. The lack of effective legal representation means that many children who might be eligible for release remain for months in detention, while others are deported back to countries in which they may face political persecution.[127] Denial of such crucial rights would be disastrous for any group, but it is particularly disastrous for children, who are at a uniquely vulnerable stage of their lives.

The denial of these fundamental rights is particularly shameful in a country like the United States, which prides itself on its respect for international human rights norms. And the blame for this situation falls squarely on the U.S. government, and in particular on the INS, which has demonstrated incompetence, neglect and bad faith in addressing the needs and rights of detained children. Many INS officials we spoke with were indifferent to the issue, while some deliberately sought to obstruct our attempts to monitor conditions. In Arizona, for example, our efforts to speak with detained children were met with suspicion and hostility, and it was only after numerous phone calls and meetings that we were finally permitted access. Even then, our work was hampered by the imposition of an arbitrary ten-minute time limit on interviews.

Before beginning our on-site investigations, we met with a number of high-level INS officials in Washington, DC. We were repeatedly assured by these officials that the INS had a national commitment to child welfare. "Our goal is not to have custody for long . . . . We handle these kids in a very special manner," said Elizabeth Herskovitz, a detention and deportation officer in Washington. Ken Elwood, the INS acting chief enforcement officer for field operations, reaffirmed this: "We're trying to professionalize and set up a non-punitive atmosphere . . . . We want to get kids through the process quickly, and if we can't get them out right away, we want to put them in shelter-care or foster care, so that we at least get them into a non-restrictive setting."[128]

---

[127] The *"refoulement"* (return) of refugees to the countries from which they have fled violates international law.

[128] Human Rights Watch meeting with Arthur Strathern, Alexander Aleinikoff, executive associate commissioner for programs, Elizabeth Herskovitz, detention and deportation division, Ken Elwood, acting chief enforcement officer, Field Operations, and Rubén Cortines, director of the Detention Management Branch, in Washington, D.C., April

Washington INS officials were sanguine about detention conditions for children: "We pay a lot to keep them in safe, wholesome facilities," Arthur Strathern, an attorney with the INS General Counsel's Office, told us. He went on to assure us that any child in custody for more than seventy-two hours would be placed in a shelter-care facility rather than a juvenile detention center, and that when placed temporarily in detention centers, "our juveniles are segregated completely [from convicted offenders]. They have completely different programs. The programs just happen to be located in the sites where offenders are. . . . [Places like Los Padrinos] comply with all the regulations: they provide books, counseling, recreation, support, etcetera." Officials painted a similarly rosy picture when it came to access to counsel. Rubén Cortines, the INS director of detention management, told us that children are never transferred without notification: "The attorneys know right away where the kids have gone. We've never had any complaints from attorneys. They have no problem getting access to the kids."[129]

As the preceding sections of this report make clear, none of these statements were borne out by our investigations. And while the misinformation we were given by officials in Washington may result from ignorance rather than bad faith, it is nonetheless difficult to excuse. Top-level INS officials have an obligation to make sure that regional offices comply with U.S. law and with INS policies.

Even less excusable was the level of ignorance that seemed to prevail among top INS officials at a regional level. In Los Angeles, Rosemary Melville, the INS Acting District Director, told us that "We have a very open environment with local attorneys. They're given policy changes and everything, and have lots of access to the kids. . . . We're all concerned with the welfare of the kids. . . As far as we know, all our facilities are up to the *Flores* standards. . . Access to phones and representation is no problem for the kids."[130]

When pressed for details on national and district policies relating to unaccompanied minors, however, Ms. Melville appeared unaware of many of the most basic legal requirements and of the actual circumstances in which minors are detained in Los Angeles. Ms. Melville said she did not know what would happen

---

15, 1996.

[129] Ibid.

[130] Human Rights Watch interviews with Rosemary Melville, Acting District Director of the INS, Los Angeles District, and Leonard Kovensky, Acting Deputy District Director, April 18 and April 24, 1996.

to an unrepresented minor under the age of sixteen at a deportation hearing. She was unsure whether or not minors held in Los Angeles County detention centers are always kept separate from convicted offenders (they are not), and equally uncertain about whether the INS had any policy about separation from offenders (there is a policy, and it states that INS minor detainees should be segregated from offenders). John Salter, the Los Angeles INS District Counsel, was similarly uninformed: "There may be an INS policy . . . I don't know." When we asked how the Los Angeles district INS ensured that minors passing through the B-18 staging area made telephone calls as required by *Perez-Funez*, Mr. Salter was vague: "Maybe Detention and Deportation documents that . . . I don't know." [131]

When asked about circumstances in which minors might be released to area shelters or to foster families rather than placed in INS detention, Salter and Melville were equally uncertain. "I don't know," said Ms. Melville: "Again, I'm not an expert on this." Mr. Salter stated firmly that no minors could be released, except to immediate relatives, "without a directive from Washington. A home-study would be required, and it would be up to Washington." We pointed out that on the contrary, the regulations permit children to be released to shelters, lawyers or foster families at "the discretion of the District Director"—who was, in this case, Rosemary Melville. Ms. Melville appeared unfamiliar with this release option, and Mr. Salter asserted that the regulations permit such discretionary releases "only in 'extraordinary circumstances'—that's what the regulations say."[132]

This is inaccurate; the Western Region's regulations did indeed say this until the mid-eighties, when the *Flores* litigation led to the adoption of a national policy to replace the old policy, precisely because the old policy was deemed overly restrictive. The regulations were reworded, and the word "extraordinary" was deliberately removed, and replaced by the phrase "unusual and compelling," which was meant to be a more flexible standard for discretionary releases. While the change may appear trivial, it was made deliberately to discourage local INS officials from applying the regulations in an excessively rigid manner. The distinction was lost on Mr. Salter, however: when we drew his attention to the current wording of the regulations, he shrugged and said, "'Extraordinary,' 'unusual. . . .' What difference does it make?"[133]

---

[131] Human Rights Watch interview with Rosemary Melvile, Acting District Director of the INS, Los Angeles District, and John Salter, District Counsel, April 25, 1996.

[132] Ibid.

[133] Ibid.

More troubling than the high level of ignorance we encountered in INS officials was their attitude towards children in detention and their advocates. In Los Angeles, INS officials appeared cavalier about the fate of juvenile detainees. When we asked Rosemary Melville if she would consider looking into alternatives to detention, such as foster care and release to local shelters, she said that she had "no plans to look into anything like that." She acknowledged that she had not notified any local immigration attorneys of the change in policy resulting in the transfer of their clients and potential clients to Arizona, and she only reluctantly agreed to bring the issue up at a future meeting with attorneys.[134]   Leonard Kovensky, the Los Angeles acting assistant district director, told us, "We inform attorneys of client transfers when we have the luxury to do so."[135] Ms. Melville finally told us bluntly that "our priority is dealing with the immigration business at hand. You don't understand how busy this place gets. Kids make up only a few of our detainees and we can't spend all our time worrying about minor procedural things."[136] District Counsel John Salter also defended procedural violations on the grounds that officials needed to "save time," and when asked whether he thought non-Spanish speaking children ought to get translations of legal materials and rights advisories, he simply shrugged: "It's not in the regulations."[137]

Narcisco Leggs, the Los Angeles juvenile coordinator and the official in charge of the B-18 staging area, revealed his attitude towards detainees in a telling analogy: "I think of [the staging area] as being a kind of warehouse. We have shipping and receiving. Only it's human beings in the warehouse." Leggs refused to provide us with a clear policy on who, if anyone, might spend the night in the staging area; after first insisting that no one ever spent the night, he finally acknowledged that "when people come in after midnight, they might stay here," and that women with small children might be held in B-18 for up to twenty-four hours if they arrived after midnight. When we asked if unaccompanied children would ever be overnight, Leggs responded by saying, without elaboration, that

---

[134] Ibid.

[135] Human Rights Watch interview with Leonard Kovensky, Acting Deputy District Director of the INS, Los Angeles District, April 18, 1996.

[136] Human Rights Watch interview with Rosemary Melville, Acting District Director of the INS, Los Angeles District, April 25, 1996.

[137] Human Rights Watch interview with John Salter, Los Angeles District Counsel, April 25, 1996.

"the people who belong here stay here," and he repeatedly referred to INS detainees as "the prisoners."[138]

INS officials , like officials in many other government agencies, are often overworked and under great pressure. Nonetheless, however busy and stressful regional INS offices may become, INS officials remain obligated to protect the rights of detained minors, as required by both United States law and international standards. To the extent that the rights of children are violated because the responsible INS officials are too overworked to attend properly to the children's needs, the INS should re-assign personnel so that an adequate number of staff are available to ensure that detained children do not continue to slip between the cracks.

If INS officials in Los Angeles were characterized by ignorance and indifference towards detained children, officials in Arizona distinguished themselves by what often appeared to be overt ill-will towards detained children and their advocates. In Los Angeles, we did encounter some difficulties in gaining access to facilities and in having confidential discussions with children, but the difficulties seemed a matter of passive resistance. In Arizona, however, we met with active hostility. INS officials and their agents at the detention facility seemed determined to prevent us from gaining access to accurate information about the children in their custody. We encountered everything from the standard forms of bureaucratic resistance[139] to transparent and deliberate falsehoods, along with a wide variety of blatantly obstructive behavior. For instance, officials told us falsely that all detained children had legal representatives. In some cases, officials actually gave to public interest attorneys the names of organizations they claimed were representing children, but when we checked this information we found that attorneys at the organizations concerned had had no contact with the children or the facility. In other instances, officials refused to provide us with the names of the attorneys claimed to be representing the children, despite the fact that this is public information.

---

[138] Interview with Narcisco Leggs, INS Los Angeles District juvenile coordinator and head of staging area, April 23, 1996. According to local public interest attorneys, there have been instances in which mothers with small children have been held in B-18 for several days at a stretch; such allegations form the basis of a recent lawsuit filed by CARECEN against the Los Angeles District of the INS. (Human Rights Watch interview with Judy London, CARECEN, April 22, 1996).

[139] Telephone calls went unreturned, memos were deliberately misconstrued, and previous requests and understandings were "forgotten."

Similarly, when we requested a copy of the Arizona facility's written policy on access to courts and legal information (the existence of which is required by INS regulations) we were at first told that no such policy existed.[140] Ultimately, Melissa Jenkins, then-director of the facility, told us that she had a copy but refused to give it to us.[141] She and her staff likewise refused to provide us with a copy of the facility rules or a copy of the free legal services list, both of which, by INS regulations, must be given to the children.[142] These refusals to cooperate with our reasonable requests were witnessed and acquiesced to by two Phoenix District INS officials: Annie López, the juvenile coordinator, and Jim Barrett, the detention and deportation Supervisor. No reasons were offered for the withholding of this basic information.

This hostility appears to characterize Southwest Key's and the INS's relationship with outside groups generally. Other organizations also report difficulties in gaining access to the Arizona facility. For instance, attorneys from TECLA, the only local organization that offers legal services to indigent detained minors, were repeatedly refused access to the facility for the purpose of making rights presentations to the children. Similarly, refugee and immigrant advocacy organizations have been denied access. The Women's Commission for Refugee Women and Children, for example, repeatedly requested permission to enter two facilities where juveniles were held and were repeatedly put off in their requests. The INS's rationale was that the INS was being sued for the detention of minors, was in the process of settling that lawsuit, and that visits by NGOs were "disruptive."[143]

The INS justifies keeping children in remote, high-security facilities on the grounds that some of the Chinese children may be at risk of being kidnaped or harmed by the smugglers who initially brought them to the United States. Evaluating this problem is beyond the scope of this report. It seems, however, that the INS and Southwest Key use the threat of interference from smugglers as an excuse for keeping all of the children completely out of the public eye. While this

---

[140] Human Rights Watch interview with Melissa Jenkins, Sheila Prosser, Annie López, and Jim Barrett, Southwest Key facility, May 21, 1996.

[141] Ibid.

[142] Ibid.

[143] Mary Diaz, Director of the Women's Commission for Refugee Women and Children, e-mail communication, March 3, 1997.

may protect some of the Chinese children from harm, it also has the effect of preventing *all* of the detained children from getting access to those who might help them.

Accompanying this resistance to the work of Human Rights Watch and other organizations was what appeared to be hostility towards the children in detention. Local attorneys told us that children complained that facility staff were "mean" and that on at least one occasion staff members pushed them around. Two boys reported, for instance, that one Southwest Key staff member, angry that they had not responded to him quickly enough, "flipped" them from their beds by yanking one side of their mattresses up in the air.[144] Despite their full knowledge of the stringent regulatory requirements governing the Arizona facility, staff discouraged children from contacting lawyers, refused to permit frequent or confidential telephone calls, and failed to provide children with required field trips, library access, and religious worship opportunities. This pattern of violations of the children's rights was ongoing as of December, despite repeated complaints from local attorneys, pointed questioning from Human Rights Watch, and knowledge of the violations by INS and Southwest Key officials. Under the circumstances, it is impossible not to conclude that the ongoing violations are deliberate, and that the INS is knowingly permitting these violations to occur.

We have heard reports of even more serious abuses by the INS. The INS currently has arrangements with several agencies throughout the country to provide "shelter care" for detained unaccompanied minors. In this report, we discuss the problems we found at the facility in Arizona, which is operated by Southwest Key. Because of time and budgetary constraints, we were unable to make a through investigation of conditions at other INS juvenile detention facilities. As this report was going to press, however, we were contacted by an employee at one of the juvenile centers we have not yet investigated, who informed us that children in that facility are being physically abused by some of the staff.[145] We have received scattered reports of similar abuses in other facilities as well. At this time, we cannot assess the credibility of these reports, but given the existing evidence of INS malfeasance, these allegations urgently require further investigation.

Similarly, a number of individuals and agencies have told us that the worst rights violations often occur during the first seventy-two hours of

---

[144] This incident was being investigated by the Justice Department's Office of the Inspector General.

[145] This employee spoke to us on the understanding that we would not quote her directly or reveal her identity.

detention—during which period   the INS is free to place minors virtually anywhere—and during the deportation process.[146] We heard numerous stories of children being arrested during INS "sweeps" of communities, being verbally and physically threatened and abused, and being literally dumped across the Mexican border in the middle of the night. In the 1993 Supreme Court case *Flores V. Reno*, the INS told the court that they arrest about 8500 children each year[147], but at any one time, only 200 to 300 are in long-term detention. This leaves the fate of thousands of children unknown. Some are presumably released to relatives, and others accept voluntary departure, but the INS claims not to track children who are released, deported, or who accept voluntary departure within seventy-two hours.[148] In the absence of reliable and publicly available records, it is impossible to determine what happens to these children while in the hands of the INS. As a result, the truth of these allegations is likewise difficult to assess, but this issue too requires further investigation.

---

[146] Human Rights Watch interview with Carlos Holguin, Center for Human Rights and Constitutional Law, Los Angeles, and Claudia Smith, California Rural Legal Assistance, Oceanside, April 19, 1996.

[147] *Flores v. Reno*, 113 S.Ct. 1439,1443 (1993)(Quoting INS briefs). This number may have increased, but since the INS. claims not to keep statistics on the number of children apprehended each year, we were unable to obtain accurate figures for more recent years.

[148] According to the United Nations High Commissioner for Refugees, "Accurate statistics on unaccompanied children should be kept and updated periodically. These should be disseminated amongst relevant agencies and authorities. . . ." UNHCR Note on Policies and Procedures in dealing with Unaccompanied Children Seeking Asylum, Section 5.19.

VI. CONCLUSION

Unlike most other government agencies, the INS occupies a dual role: it exists to provide a service to visitors, immigrants and asylum seekers, but it also exists to enforce United States immigration laws. Much of the time, however, INS officials and employees appear to forget their role as service providers, and instead structure their professional identities around their role as law enforcement agents. Thus, administrative detainees become "the prisoners" -a phrase we heard with distressing frequency from INS officials at all levels- and few INS officials question the notion that unaccompanied minors may be kept in prison-like conditions. This situation is exacerbated by the lack of independent oversight for the INS. "Service" is a forgotten concept: in the frank words of David Tally, of the INS Western Region counsel's office, "We're here to deport people, if they're deportable."[149]

More than any other group of aliens, unaccompanied children suffer as a result of this attitude, for it creates a grave conflict of interest for the INS. Unlike adults, unaccompanied children cannot simply be left to fend for themselves while their immigration status is being adjudicated. Both United States law and international standards reflect an awareness that children require special protection and care. This means that unaccompanied children apprehended by the INS must be placed in the custody of some responsible adult or agency: children need food, housing, medical care, counseling, education and many other things that they are too young to obtain on their own. And children going through deportation or exclusion hearings as a result of INS apprehension also need legal assistance, since their young age, the complexity of immigration proceedings, and their frequent lack of English skills makes it almost impossible for them to obtain a fair hearing without the help of an attorney. This points to a need for the children to be placed in the care of individuals or agencies capable of protecting the children's rights and interests.

The INS, by definition, is not such an agency. Much of the time, the interests of the INS run directly contrary to the interests of detained children: in deportation and exclusion hearings, for instance, the children and the INS are adversarial parties. The INS and its agents have little structural incentive to protect

---

[149] Human Rights Watch interview with David Tally, Western Region General Counsel's Office, May 22, 1996. This comment was echoed by Jim Barrett, the INS Phoenix district supervisor for detention and deportation, who told us that "The INS's goal is to get these kids into deportation proceedings." Human Rights Watch interview with Jim Barrett, INS Phoenix district supervisor for detention and deportation, May 21, 1996.

the children's rights, and many incentives to overlook their rights. Detained alien children are powerless and alone, and often no one but the INS is even aware of their presence in the United States. There are few mechanisms for effective monitoring of the INS, and as a result, the INS today remains free to violate children's rights with impunity.

Other nations have dealt with this conflict of interest by separating the care-taking agency from the agency charged with the prosecution of unaccompanied minors.[150] Thus, in the United Kingdom, unaccompanied children are placed in the care of local authority social service departments.[151] In the Netherlands, such children are cared for by a nongovernmental organization called De Opbouw, which assumes guardianship of the children; the Dutch government pays for the cost of the children's care.[152] In Denmark, too, unaccompanied alien children are cared for by nongovernmental organizations.[153] In Canada, the children are placed in the care of a government child welfare agency, either the Children's Aid Society or the Ministry of Social Services.[154]

This separation of the care-taking functions from the prosecution functions is a simple and natural method of eliminating the built-in conflict of interest that now causes so many problems for unaccompanied children in the United States. Human Rights Watch therefore recommends that once children are apprehended

---

[150] The United Nations High Commissioner for Refugees recommends that all unaccompanied children have a guardian or adviser appointed from "an independent and formally accredited organization" in each country: "The guardian or adviser should have the necessary expertise in the field of childcaring, so as to ensure that the interests of the child are safe-guarded, and that the child's legal, social, medical and psychological nedds are appropriately covered. . . ." Note on Policies, section 5.7. This lends further support to the view that care-taking should be done by an independent child-welfare agency capable of protecting the children's interests, rather than by the INS.

[151] Letter, Louise Williamson, Director, Children's Division, The Refugee Council, London, February 14, 1997.

[152] Human Rights Watch telephone interview with Elspeth Faber, De Opbouw, November 11, 1996.

[153] Human Rights Watch telephone interview with Johanna Djurhuus, consultant on unaccompanied Children for the Danish Refugee Council, November 11, 1996.

[154] Human Rights Watch telephone interview with Agnes Casselman, Director of International Social Services, Canada, November 11, 1996.

by the INS, they should be placed in the care of appropriate child welfare authorities, rather than in detention facilities run by the INS or its agents.

Until such time as the INS relinquishes its care-taking functions, the agency should take steps to abide by the law and eliminate current abuses. Conditions in detention facilities could easily be improved; for one thing, contracting with experienced child welfare organizations rather than with organizations specializing in the operation of detention centers for juvenile delinquents would likely lead towards a less punitive environment in detention facilities.

Experience thus far confirms this view: in the Chicago area, for instance, an agency called the Heartland Alliance is under contract to the INS to provide shelter-care for unaccompanied children. Unlike Southwest Key, the company that runs the Arizona detention facility, the Heartland Alliance is not in the business of running detention centers for juvenile delinquents; instead, it has long been a respected part of Chicago's social service community. And the difference shows: local attorneys report hearing no complaints about conditions at the Chicago facility, and a brief site visit by Human Rights Watch appeared to confirm that the facility is run by a caring, well-trained, and committed staff. The Chicago facility is not free from problems; given the dearth of local lawyers able to provide free legal assistance, many children receive inadequate or no legal assistance, and staff members and local attorneys express misgivings about INS policies for dealing with the children sent to the facility. Nonetheless, conditions in Chicago appear to be significantly better than conditions in Los Angeles or Arizona.

Similarly, past experiences in a number of cities suggest that releasing children to unrelated adult friends or to local foster families often provides a viable alternative to detention. The cost of keeping a child in detention is roughly $100 a day,[155] a figure which seems insignificant relative to the overall INS budget, which is $3.1 billion for 1997 alone.[156] Foster care can be a great deal cheaper, and releasing children to unrelated family friends is at virtually no expense to the government. The INS claims that placing unaccompanied children in such settings may expose them to the risk of kidnappings or reprisals by smugglers. But while

---

[155] Human Rights Watch interveiw with Alexander Aleinikoff, executive associate commissioner for programs; Ruben Cortina, director of detention management branch, Detention and Deportation Division; Elizabeth Herskovitz, detention and deportation officer; Ken Elwood, INS acting chief enforcement officer, Field Operations; and Arthur Strathern.

[156] *Arizona Daily Star*, January 15, 1997, p. 8.

some children (especially those from China) may indeed be at risk, the possible danger to some children should not be used to justify unnecessary restrictions on the freedom of all the children. If some children must be kept in secure facilities for their own safety, this should be determined on a case by case basis, and long-term detention should only be resorted to when there has been an individualized determination that no other option will ensure a child's safety.

In order to ensure that the rights of children are protected, the INS should keep comprehensive records on all unaccompanied children it apprehends,[157] and should cooperate with outside groups wishing to monitor conditions or provide assistance to detained children. Finally, any unaccompanied children who remain in INS detention while their immigration status is being resolved should receive government appointed lawyers if they are too poor to pay for an attorney themselves.

Unlike many problems facing the INS today, the problem of minors in detention is solvable. Relatively small numbers of children are involved (an average of 200 to 300 children in longer-term custody at any given time), and the total cost of caring for the children and providing them with legal assistance is insignificant relative to the overall INS budget. INS administrative detention for minors is in many cases avoidable; when unavoidable, there is no reason for that detention to be punitive. That it be not only punitive, but fraught with illegalities as well, is inexcusable.

---

[157] These statistics should be made available to the general public. They should also be provided to the United Nations High Commissioner for Refugees, as required by Article 35 of the United Nations Convention on the Status of Refugees and by Article II of the United Nations Protocol on the Status of Refugees. The "Recommendations" section of this report provides details on the nature of the statistics that should be kept. Keeping such comprehensive records is especially crucial for protecting the rights of those children detained for fewer than seventy-two hours, about whom little is currently known.

APPENDICES

APPENDIX A
SELECTED ARTICLES FROM THE U.N. CONVENTION ON THE RIGHTS OF THE CHILD

Convention on the Rights of the Child, G.A. res. 44/25, annex, 44 U.N. GAOR Supp. (No. 49) at 167, U.N. Doc. A/44/49 (1989).

Preamble

The States Parties to the present Convention,

Considering that, in accordance with the principles proclaimed in the Charter of the United Nations, recognition of the inherent dignity and of the equal and inalienable rights of all members of the human family is the foundation of freedom, justice and peace in the world,

Bearing in mind that the peoples of the United Nations have, in the Charter, reaffirmed their faith in fundamental human rights and in the dignity and worth of the human person, and have determined to promote social progress and better standards of life in larger freedom,

Recognizing that the United Nations has, in the Universal Declaration of Human Rights and in the International Covenants on Human Rights, proclaimed and agreed that everyone is entitled to all the rights and freedoms set forth therein, without distinction of any kind, such as race, colour, sex, language, religion, political or other opinion, national or social origin, property, birth or other status,

Recalling that, in the Universal Declaration of Human Rights, the United Nations has proclaimed that childhood is entitled to special care and assistance,

Convinced that the family, as the fundamental group of society and the natural environment for the growth and well-being of all its members and particularly children, should be afforded the necessary protection and assistance so that it can fully assume its responsibilities within the community,

Recognizing that the child, for the full and harmonious development of his or her personality, should grow up in a family environment, in an atmosphere of happiness, love and understanding,

Considering that the child should be fully prepared to live an individual life in society, and brought up in the spirit of the ideals proclaimed in the Charter of the

United Nations, and in particular in the spirit of peace, dignity, tolerance, freedom, equality and solidarity,

Bearing in mind that the need to extend particular care to the child has been stated in the Geneva Declaration of the Rights of the Child of 1924 and in the Declaration of the Rights of the Child adopted by the General Assembly on 20 November 1959 and recognized in the Universal Declaration of Human Rights, in the International Covenant on Civil and Political Rights (in particular in articles 23 and 24), in the International Covenant on Economic, Social and Cultural Rights (in particular in article 10) and in the statutes and relevant instruments of specialized agencies and international organizations concerned with the welfare of children,

Bearing in mind that, as indicated in the Declaration of the Rights of the Child, "the child, by reason of his physical and mental immaturity, needs special safeguards and care, including appropriate legal protection, before as well as after birth,"

Recalling the provisions of the Declaration on Social and Legal Principles relating to the Protection and Welfare of Children, with Special Reference to Foster Placement and Adoption Nationally and Internationally; the United Nations Standard Minimum Rules for the Administration of Juvenile Justice (The Beijing Rules) ; and the Declaration on the Protection of Women and Children in Emergency and Armed Conflict,

Recognizing that, in all countries in the world, there are children living in exceptionally difficult conditions, and that such children need special consideration,

Taking due account of the importance of the traditions and cultural values of each people for the protection and harmonious development of the child,

Recognizing the importance of international co-operation for improving the living conditions of children in every country, in particular in the developing countries, have agreed as follows:

Part I
Article 1
For the purposes of the present Convention, a child means every human being below the age of eighteen years unless under the law applicable to the child, majority is attained earlier.

Article 2

1. States Parties shall respect and ensure the rights set forth in the present Convention to each child within their jurisdiction without discrimination of any kind, irrespective of the child's or his or her parent's or legal guardian's race, colour, sex, language, religion, political or other opinion, national, ethnic or social origin, property, disability, birth or other status.

2. States Parties shall take all appropriate measures to ensure that the child is protected against all forms of discrimination or punishment on the basis of the status, activities, expressed opinions, or beliefs of the child's parents, legal guardians, or family members.

Article 3

1. In all actions concerning children, whether undertaken by public or private social welfare institutions, courts of law, administrative authorities or legislative bodies, the best interests of the child shall be a primary consideration.

2. States Parties undertake to ensure the child such protection and care as is necessary for his or her well-being, taking into account the rights and duties of his or her parents, legal guardians, or other individuals legally responsible for him or her, and, to this end, shall take all appropriate legislative and administrative measures.

3. States Parties shall ensure that the institutions, services and facilities responsible for the care or protection of children shall conform with the standards established by competent authorities, particularly in the areas of safety, health, in the number and suitability of their staff, as well as competent supervision.

Article 22

1. States Parties shall take appropriate measures to ensure that a child who is seeking refugee status or who is considered a refugee in accordance with applicable international or domestic law and procedures shall, whether unaccompanied or accompanied by his or her parents or by any other person, receive appropriate protection and humanitarian assistance in the enjoyment of applicable rights set forth in the present Convention and in other international human rights or humanitarian instruments to which the said States are Parties.

2.   For this purpose, States Parties shall provide, as they consider appropriate, co-operation in any efforts by the United Nations and other competent intergovernmental organizations or non-governmental organizations co-operating with the United Nations to protect and assist such a child and to trace the parents or other members of the family of any refugee child in order to obtain information necessary for reunification with his or her family. In cases where no parents or other members of the family can be found, the child shall be accorded the same protection as any other child permanently or temporarily deprived of his or her family environment for any reason , as set forth in the present Convention.

Article 37
States Parties shall ensure that:

a) No child shall be subjected to torture or other cruel, inhuman or degrading treatment or punishment. Neither capital punishment nor life imprisonment without possibility of release shall be imposed for offenses committed by persons below eighteen years of age;

b) No child shall be deprived of his or her liberty unlawfully or arbitrarily. The arrest, detention or imprisonment of a child shall be in conformity with the law and shall be used only as a measure of last resort and for the shortest appropriate period of time;

c) Every child deprived of liberty shall be treated with humanity and respect for the inherent dignity of the human person, and in a manner which takes into account the needs of persons of his or her age. In particular, every child deprived of liberty shall be separated from adults unless it is considered in the child's best interest not to do so and shall have the right to maintain contact with his or her family through correspondence and visits, save in exceptional circumstances;

d) Every child deprived of his or her liberty shall have the right to prompt access to legal and other appropriate assistance, as well as the right to challenge the legality of the deprivation of his or her liberty before a court or other competent, independent and impartial authority, and to a prompt decision on any such action.

APPENDIX B
UNITED NATIONS HIGH COMMISSIONER FOR REFUGEES
NOTE ON POLICIES AND PROCEDURES IN DEALING
WITH UNACCOMPANIED CHILDREN SEEKING ASYLUM

I. Introduction

1.1   In recent years, States have expressed concern about unaccompanied children seeking asylum either at their borders or at some later time after entry. The circumstances in which these particularly vulnerable individuals find themselves are varied and often complex. Some may be in fear of persecution, human rights abuse or civil unrest in their home countries. Others may have been sent, willingly or otherwise, to secure a better future in what their caregivers have perceived to be more developed countries. In others, the motives and reasons may be mixed.

1.2   Notwithstanding any of these motives, unaccompanied children have often had little or no choice in the decisions that have led to their predicament and vulnerability. Irrespective of their immigration status, they have special needs that must be met.

1.3   The recommendations set out below should be applied in conjunction with the UNHCR Guidelines on Refugee Children. The purpose of this note is three-fold: to promote awareness of special needs of unaccompanied children and the rights reflected in the Convention on the Rights of the Child; to highlight the importance of a comprehensive approach; and to stimulate internal discussions in each country on how to develop principles and practices that will ensure that needs of unaccompanied children are being met.

1.4   Receiving countries have responded to the plight of these children through a range of governmental and non-governmental activities. Nonetheless, UNHCR considers it imperative to ensure that effective protection and assistance is delivered to unaccompanied children in a systematic, comprehensive, and integrated way. This will inevitably require the close cooperation of a variety of government bodies, specialized agencies and individuals in delivering an effective continuum of care and protection.

1.5   For this reason, UNHCR embraces the universal, cardinal principles of child care and protection that are embodied in the Convention on the

75

Rights of the Child, in particular, Article 3 paragraph 1 which provides that:

> In all actions concerning children, whether undertaken by public or private social welfare institutions, courts of law, administrative authorities or legislative bodies, the best interests of the child shall be a primary consideration.

2. International standards

2.1   In the treatment of issues concerning unaccompanied children seeking asylum, the following are the main international standards which should be taken into account: (For more exhaustive list, see Annex I.)
—Convention relating to the Status of Refugees, 1951
—Protocol relating to the Status of Refugees, 1967
—Convention on the Rights of the Child, 1989

2.2   In addition, it is recommended that the UNHCR Guidelines "Refugee Children—Guidelines on Protection and Care" (1994) be consulted.

3. Definitions
Unaccompanied child
3.1   An unaccompanied child is a person who is under the age of eighteen years, unless, under the law applicable to the child, majority is attained earlier and who is "separated from both parents and is not being cared for by an adult who by law or custom has responsibility to do so."

Children accompanied by adults who are not their parents
3.2   In many cases the child will be accompanied by an adult caregiver who may or may not be a relative of the child. In order to determine whether or not a child is considered unaccompanied, see Annex II for practical guidelines.

4. Access to the territory
4.1   Because of his/her vulnerability, an unaccompanied child seeking asylum should not be refused access to the territory and his/her claim should always be considered under the normal refugee determination procedure.

4.2   Upon arrival, a child should be provided with a legal representative. The claims of unaccompanied children should be examined in a manner which is both fair and age-appropriate.

5. Identification and initial action
Identification

5.1   Specific identification procedures for unaccompanied children need to be established in countries where they do not already exist. The main purposes of these procedures are two-fold: first, to find out whether or not the child is unaccompanied and second, to determine whether the child is an asylum seeker or not.

At port of entry

5.2   Identification of a child as being unaccompanied should be done immediately on arrival and on a priority basis. Where available, persons specially trained or who have otherwise the necessary experience or skills for dealing with children should be involved in this process. Children may be accompanied not by their own parents but by other relatives or other families. Care should be taken in assessing the nature and implications of those relationships. (See Annex II)

In-country

5.3   Some children may already have been living in the country when they come to the notice of the authorities. The process outlined below should apply equally to such children, taking into consideration additional experiences they may have had while living in the country of asylum. Efforts should be made to coordinate information-sharing between various agencies and individuals (including health, education and welfare agencies), so as to ensure that unaccompanied children are identified and assisted as early as possible.

5.4   When the child is classified as "unaccompanied" according to the criteria mentioned in Annex II, then the next course of action should be to establish whether the child is indeed seeking asylum in the country. If it is confirmed that the child is an asylum seeker, every effort should be made to process the examination of his/her claim as expeditiously and as child-appropriate as possible. If, on the other hand, there is no reason to believe that the child is seeking asylum or family reunion, return of the child should, in general, be facilitated. In such a case, the principle of non-discrimination stipulated in Article 2, the 'best interests' provision in Article 3 of the Convention on the Rights of the Child, as well as similar safeguards mentioned under the section REPATRIATION (10.12) should be taken into consideration.

Split families

5.5   There may be a situation where families are split between countries. If one of the child's parents is in another asylum country, every effort should be made to reunite the child with that parent at an early stage before status determination takes place.

Registration/documentation

5.6   Unaccompanied children should be registered through interviews. (For more details, see 5.8-5.16) In addition to the initial registration of basic biographical data, the dossier should include a social history of the child which should be compiled over time and must accompany the child whenever there is a transfer of his/her location or care arrangements. Effective documentation of the child, his/her story and all relevant information will help to ensure that subsequent actions are taken in the 'best interests' of the child.

Appointment of a guardian or adviser

5.7   It is suggested that an independent and formally accredited organization be identified/established in each country, which will appoint a guardian or adviser as soon as the unaccompanied child is identified. The guardian or adviser should have the necessary expertise in the field of childcaring, so as to ensure that the interests of the child are safeguarded, and that the child's legal, social, medical and psychological needs are appropriately covered during the refugee status determination procedures and until a durable solution for the child has been identified and implemented. To this end, the guardian or adviser would act as a link between the child and existing specialist agencies/individuals who would provide the continuum of care required by the child.

Initial interviews

5.8   Initial interviews of unaccompanied children to collect biodata and social history information should be done immediately after arrival and in an age-appropriate manner. The information should be updated periodically.

This is essential for subsequent action to determine the status of the child and to promote durable solutions.

5.9   Apart from the child's general bio-data, it is desirable that the following additional information be recorded:

a) Family information (in the country of origin and elsewhere)
b) Information on non-family members important to the child
c) Circumstances when the child was found/identified
d) Information concerning the child's separation from the family
e) Information about the child's life before and since the separation
f) Child's physical condition health and past medical history
g) Educational background (formal and informal)
h) Present care arrangements
i) Child's wishes and plans for the future
j)   Preliminary assessment of the child's mental and emotional development and maturity
k) Age assessment (See 5.11)

5.10   The guidelines contained in UNHCR's "Working with Unaccompanied Children: A Community-Based Approach" can be used as a guiding document in the data gathering exercise. "Interviewing Applicants for Refugee Status" also provides useful guidance with regard to interviewing children.

Age assessment

5.11   If an assessment of the child's age is necessary, the following considerations should be noted:

a) Such an assessment should take into account not only the physical appearance of the child but also his/her psychological maturity.

b) When scientific procedures are used in order to determine the age of the child, margins of error should be allowed. Such methods must be safe and respect human dignity.

c) The child should be given the benefit of the doubt if the exact age is uncertain. Where possible, the legal consequences or significance of the age criteria should be reduced or downplayed. It is not desirable that too many legal advantages and disadvantages are known to flow from the criteria because this may be an incentive for misrepresentation. The guiding principle is whether an individual demonstrates an "immaturity" and vulnerability that may require more sensitive treatment.

Interviewers

5.12   It is desirable that all interviews with unaccompanied children (including the interview for the determination of refugee status) should be carried out by professionally qualified and specially trained persons with appropriate knowledge of the psychological, emotional and physical development and behaviour of children. When possible, such experts should have the same cultural background and mother tongue as the child.

Interpreters

5.13   Insofar as possible, interpreters should be skilled and trained in refugee and children's issues.

Consultation

5.14   Children should be kept informed in an age-appropriate manner, about the procedures, what decisions have been made about them, and the possible consequences of their refugee status. This consultation and advice is particularly important when a durable solution is sought and implemented.

Views and wishes of the child

5.15   In all cases, the views and wishes of the child should be elicited and considered, as stipulated in the Convention on the Rights of the Child Article 12 paragraph 1:

> States Parties shall assure to the child who is capable of forming his or her views the right to express those views freely in all matters affecting the child, the views of the child being given due weight in accordance with the age and maturity of the child.

Confidentiality

5.16   In obtaining, sharing and preserving the information collected, particular care must be taken in order not to endanger the well-being of persons still within the child's country of origin, especially the child's family members. Care must be taken that information sought and shared for one purpose is not inappropriately used for another purpose.

Tracing

5.17   Tracing for parents or families is essential and should begin as soon as possible. To that end, the services of the National Red Cross or Red Crescent Societies and the International Commitee of the Red Cross (ICRC) should be requested where necessary. In cases where there may be a threat to the life or integrity of a child or its close relatives, particularly if they have remained in their country of origin, care must be taken to ensure that the collection, processing and circulation of information concerning those persons is undertaking on a confidential basis, so as to avoid jeopardizing their safety.

Tracking

5.18   It is important to keep track of each unaccompanied child (location, care arrangements, etc) in order to ensure that each child receives appropriate care and to avoid any risk of abuse taking place. Where possible, UNHCR recommends the establishment of a centralized electronic register that can be regularly updated as the child's legal and social status evolves.

Statistics

5.19   Accurate statistics on unaccompanied children should be kept and updated periodically. These should be disseminated amongst relevant agencies and authorities in the interest of information-sharing and network-building.

6. Access to asylum procedures
Children should be entitled to access to asylum procedures, regardless of their age.

7. Interim care and protection of children seeking asylum
General
7.1   Children seeking asylum, particularly if they are unaccompanied, are entitled to special care and protection.

Care and accommodation
7.2   In order to ensure continuity of care and bearing in mind the best interests of the child, changes in residence for unaccompanied children should be limited to a minimum.

7.3   Siblings should be kept together in conformity with the principle of family unity.

7.4   A child who has adult relatives arriving together or already living in the country of asylum should be allowed to stay with them, pending determination of his/her status. In view of the child's vulnerability and the potential for abuse, regular assessments should be made by the appropriate social welfare authorities.

7.5   Whether they are accommodated in foster homes or special reception centres, children seeking asylum, should be under regular supervision and assessment by qualified persons, to ensure their physical and psychosocial well-being.

Detention

7.6   Children seeking asylum should not be kept in detention. This is particularly important in the case of unaccompanied children.

7.7   States which, regrettably and contrary to the preceding recommendation, may keep children seeking asylum in detention, should, in any event, observe Article 37 of the Convention of the Rights of the Child, according to which detention shall be used only as a measure of last resort and for the shortest appropriate period of time. If children who are asylum seekers are detained in airports, immigration-holding centres or prisons, they must not be held under prison-like conditions. All efforts must be made to have them released from detention and placed in other appropriate accommodation. If this proves impossible, special arrangements must be made for living quarters which are suitable for children and their families. The underlying approach to such a programme should be 'care' and not 'detention'. Facilities should not be located in isolated areas where culturally-appropriate community resources and legal access may be unavailable.

7.8   During detention, children have the right to education which should optimally take place outside the detention premises in order to facilitate the continuance of their education upon release. Under the UN Rules for Juveniles Deprived of their Liberty E-38, States are required to provide special education programmes to children of foreign origin with particular cultural or ethnic needs.

Health care

7.9   The Convention on the Rights of the Child declares that the child has the right to enjoy the highest attainable standard of health and facilities for the treatment of illness and rehabilitation of health. Children seeking asylum should have the same access to health care as national children. In the countries from which they have fled, basic preventive care such as immunizations and education about health, hygiene and nutrition may have been lacking; these deficiencies must be remedied in a sensitive and effective manner in the country of asylum.

7.10   Unaccompanied children have all experienced separation from family members and they have also in varying degrees experienced loss, trauma, disruption, and violence. The pervasive violence and stress of a country afflicted by war may create deep-rooted feelings of helplessness and undermine a child's trust in others. Reports constantly reflect the existence of profound trauma in many children, which calls for special sensitivity and attention in their care and rehabilitation.

7.11   The Convention on the Rights of the Child sets out the duty of states to provide rehabilitation services to children who have been victims of any form of abuse, neglect, exploitation, torture, cruel, inhuman and degrading treatment or armed conflicts. To facilitate such recovery and reintegration, culturally-appropriate mental health care should be developed and qualified psycho-social counselling be provided.

Education

7.12   Every child, regardless of status, should have full access to education in the asylum country. The child should be registered with appropriate school authorities as soon as possible.

7.13   All children seeking asylum should have the right to maintain their cultural identity and values, including the maintenance and and further development of their mother tongue.

7.14   All juveniles should be allowed to enroll in vocational/professional training or education which would improve their prospects, especially when returning to their country of origin.

8. Refugee status determination for unaccompanied children
Procedures

8.1   Considering their vulnerability and special needs, it is essential that children's refugee status applications be given priority and that every effort be made to reach a decision promptly and fairly. All appeals should be processed fairly and as expeditiously as possible.

8.2   Minimum procedural guarantees should include determination by a competent authority, fully qualified in asylum and refugee matters; where the age and maturity of the child permits, the opportunity for a personal interview with a qualified official before any final decision is made; and a possibility to appeal for a formal review of the decision.

8.3   Not being legally independent, an asylum-seeking child should be represented by an adult who is familiar with the child's background and who would protect his/her interests. Access should also be given to a qualified legal representative. This principle should apply to all children, including those between sixteen and eighteen, even where application for refugee status is processed under the normal procedures for adults.

8.4   The interviews should be conducted by specially qualified and trained representatives of the refugee determination authority who will take into account the special situation of unaccompanied children, in order to carry out the refugee status assessment.

8.5   An asylum-seeker or his/her legal representative should be able to seek a review of the decision. Appropriate deadlines should be set out for a child to appeal a negative decision. Every effort should be made to reach a decision in an efficient manner in order not to keep children in limbo for a long period of time regarding their status and their future. All appeals should be processed fairly and as expeditiously as possible. This may require children's appeals to be prioritized over other outstanding appeals.

Criteria

8.6   Although the same definition of a refugee applies to all individuals regardless of their age, in the examination of the factual elements of the claim of an unaccompanied child, particular regard should be given to circumstances such as the child's stage of development, his/her possibly limited knowledge of conditions in the country of origin, and their significance to the legal concept of refugee status, as well as his/her special vulnerability. Children may manifest their fears in ways different from adults. Therefore, in the examination of their claims, it may be necessary to have greater regard to certain objective factors, and to determine, based upon these factors, whether a child may be presumed to have a well-founded fear of persecution.

8.7   It should be further borne in mind that, under the Convention on the Rights of the Child, children are recognized certain specific human rights, and that the manner in which those rights may be violated as well as the nature of such violations may be different from those that may occur in the case of adults. Certain policies and practices constituting gross violations of specific rights of the child may, under certain circumstances, lead to situations that fall within the scope of the refugee Convention. Examples of such policies and practices are the recruitment of children for regular or irregular armies, their subjection to forced labour, the trafficking of children for prostitution and sexual exploitation and the practice of female genital mutilation.

8.8   It is also important to take into account the circumstances of the family members as this may be central to a child's refugee claim. Principles of confidentiality should not be compromised in this regard. While the child may have personally fear or have experienced persecution, more often s/he may fear or have been affected by other discriminatory or persecutory measures affecting the entire family.

8.9   Children often do not leave their country of origin on their own initiative. They are generally sent out by their parents or principal caregivers. "If there is reason to believe that the parents wish their child to be outside the country of origin on grounds of their own well-founded fear of persecution, the child him/herself may be presumed to have such a fear." If the will of the parents cannot be ascertained or if such will is in doubt, then a decision will have to be made regarding the well-foundedness of the child's fear on the basis of all known circumstances.

8.10   The final decisions should be based on a case-by-case examination of the unique combination of factors presented by each child, including the child's personal, family and cultural background. Therefore, it is important that persons involved in the refugee status determination procedures have an understanding of the history, culture and background of the child.

9. Identification of durable solution
Children who are found to qualify for asylum

9.1   If the child is granted asylum or permitted to stay on humanitarian grounds, possible durable solutions are either local integration or resettlement in a third country, normally on the grounds of family reunification. (Also see relevant paragraphs in 10. *Implementation of Durable Solution*, a. *Local integration* and c. *Resettlement)*

Children who are not found to qualify for asylum

9.2   If the child is found not to qualify for asylum, either as a refugee or on humanitarian grounds, an assessment of the solution that is in the best interests of the child should follow as soon as practicable after the negative result of his/her application is confirmed.

9.3   In order to make appropriate arrangements for return, tracing and home assessment would be of particular importance. Effective assessments may require that home assessment or tracing be conducted in the country of origin. This entails tracing the child's family and clarifying the family situation, by, for example, making an assessment of the ability of the child's family in the country of origin to receive the child and to provide appropriate care. It may also entail gauging the need for eventual material assistance to the family concerned. Information collected through tracing and home assessment can often provide a firm basis for a best interest decision with regard to the child's future. Such information could be gathered through existing NGO's which may already have presence in the country of origin and are equipped to do such activities.

9.4   The best interests of an unaccompanied child require that the child not be returned unless, prior to the return, a suitable care-giver such as a parent, other relative, other adult care-taker, a government agency, a child-care agency in the country of origin has agreed, and is able to take responsibility for the child and provide him/her with appropriate protection and care.

9.5   Special efforts must be made to ensure the provision of appropriate counselling for a child who is to be returned. This is particularly important in case of individual reluctance, as well as family pressure not to return. If possible, the child should be encouraged to communicate with his/her family members prior to return.

9.6   The possibility of using the expertise of international agencies could be explored, notably for initiating/maintaining contacts both with the child's family and with the authorities in the country of origin and establishing an assistance programme for the family, when deemed necessary and appropriate.

9.7   It is acknowledged that many different perspectives will need to be taken into account in identifying the most appropriate solution for a child who is not eligible for asylum. Such multidisciplinary approach may, for example, be ensured by the establishment of Panels in charge of considering on a case-by-case basis which solution is in the best interests of the child, and making appropriate recommendations. The composition of such Panels could be broad-based, including for instance representatives of the competent governmental departments or agencies, representatives of child welfare agencies (in particular that or those under whose care the child has been placed), and representatives of organizations or associations grouping persons of the same national origin as the child.

Criteria

9.8   In identifying a solution, all circumstances, should be taken into consideration. As a guiding concept, principles of family reunification and best interests are usually compatible. Thus, reunification with parents will generally be in the best interests of a child. However, where best interests and family reunification principles are incompatible, the best interests of the child should take precedence. Circumstances may exist which call into question the appropriateness of a child reuniting with his/her parents or other principal caregiver. Examples be where there are substantiated allegations of sexual abuse or similarly serious considerations.

10. Implementation of durable solution
General
10.1   In recognition of the particular vulnerability of unaccompanied children, every effort should be made to ensure that decisions relating to them are taken and implemented without any undue delays.

A. Local integration
10.2   As soon as the child has been recognized refugee status or permitted to stay on humanitarian grounds, long-term placement in a community should be arranged. Authorities, schools, organizations, care institutions and individuals involved in the care of the unaccompanied refugee child in the community, should co-ordinate their efforts to keep to a minimum the number of different official entities with which the child is in contact.

10.3   To facilitate the integration of the child into the host country a structured orientation programme in which the child is given a thorough explanation of his/her legal status and a brief introduction to the host culture should be provided. The information should be adapted to the age of the child.

10.4   Although the placement of a child depends on the standards and practices of each country of asylum's social welfare system, the decision should always be in the child's best interests and "without discrimination of any kind." (Art.2 of the Convention on the Rights of the Child) A careful individual assessment taking into account such factors as the child's age, sex, emotional state, family background, continuity/discontinuity of care, possibilities of family reunion, reasons for flight, educational background etc should be carried out. The UNHCR Guidelines "Working with Unaccompanied Children: A Community-Based Approach" could be an important tool for obtaining information with the view of documenting the social history of the child. It is important that the social welfare officers/reception centre staff involved have time to assess the conditions of the child and ask him/her about expectations of care before making a definite decision.

Family Tracing/Reunion
10.5   Family reunion is the first priority and it is essential that unaccompanied children are assisted in locating and communicating with their family members. Advice may be sought from the ICRC Central Tracing Agency or, if need be, from the tracing services of other international institutions.

Assitance from the national Ree Cross and Red Crescent Societies may be required to restore such links. All attempts should be made to reunite the child with his/her family or other person to whom the child is close, when the best interests of the child would be met by such a reunion. When family reunion takes place the family may have been separated for a long period of time. They must therefore be given time and support to re-establish family relationships. (See also 9.4)

Long-term placement

10.6   Children who have been living with relatives/adult friends since arrival should be allowed to continue to live with them if the social welfare authorities or another competent body has assessed that the child's needs are being met adequately. Depending on the child's age, developmental level and future family reunion possibilities the following long-term placements are recommended;

Family Care

10.7   In most cultures children less than fifteen years of age are still primarily dependent upon the family for developmental progress and guidance. When they are likely to be separated from their own parents for a longer period they should be provided the opportunity to benefit from a stable family environment. It is preferable that, whenever possible, a child should be placed in a family from his/her own culture. When a child is placed in a foster home or with relatives, a contact with the social welfare authorities should be established. Professional support is often needed, especially in the initial phase.

Group Care

10.8   Small group homes that are integrated into the host community and staffed by adults with a cultural sensitivity should be considered when placement in foster families is not feasible. Adolescents might have difficulties accepting other adults as parental figures. For them small group homes might be the best alternative, although the importance of the presence of adults to guide them in their daily life cannot be over-emphasized. The goal of a group home should not be to replicate a family but to assist adolescents to become increasingly independent and self-sufficient.

10.9   Young adults who have left their "care" environment should be given access to "after care." They should be assigned a contact person and should have access to information and advise on issues like welfare rights, housing, education etc. Such services should be available to the young adult as long as considered necessary.]

Welfare
10.10   All the children's rights, that is, legal, medical, education and others, mentioned in the Interim Care (Section 7) should be consolidated in their long-term welfare. Refugee children should be ensured all the rights stipulated in the Convention on the Rights of the Child.

B. Resettlement
10.11   When it is considered that resettlement is in the best interest of the child, generally on the ground of family reunification, swift implementation.

C. Repatriation
10.12   Should repatriation be considered as the most appropriate durable solution, the return will not be carried out unless all the conditions indicated in above paragraph 9.4 have been met and the corresponding arrangements have been made.

10.13   Special efforts must be made to ensure the provision of appropriate counselling for a child who is to be returned. This is particularly important in case of individual reluctance, as well as family pressure not to return. If possible, the child should be encouraged to communicate with his/her family members prior to return.

10.14   The possibility of using the expertise of international agencies could be explored, notably for initiating/maintaining contacts both with the child's family and with the authorities in the country of origin and establishing an assistance programme for the family, when deemed necessary and appropriate.

11. Staff training
It is desirable that agencies dealing with unaccompanied children establish special recruitment practices and training schemes, so as to ensure that persons that will assume responsibilities for the care of the children understand their needs and possess the necessary skills to help them in the most effective way.

12. Cooperation and coordination
The process above will involve information-sharing and networking between agencies and individuals from different disciplines, often with different mandates and agenda. The close cooperation of a variety of government bodies, specialized agencies and individuals in delivering an effective continuum of care is crucial.

Annex I
List of international and regional standards
—Convention relating to the Status of Refugees, 1951
—Protocol relating to the Status of Refugees, 1967
—Universal Declaration of Human Rights, 1948
—Convention relating to the Status of Stateless Persons, 1954
—International Covenant on Civil and Political Rights and Optional Protocol thereto, 1966
—International Covenant on Economic, Social and Cultural Rights, 1966
—European Convention for the Protection of Human Rights and Fundamental Freedoms and Protocols, 1950
—Hague Convention for the Protection of Minors, 1961
—Convention on the Civil Aspects of Child Abduction, 1980
—Convention on the Rights of the Child, 1989
—Hague Convention on Protection of Children and Co-operation in respect of Intercountry Adoption, 1993
—United Nations Rules for the Protection of Juveniles Deprived of Their Liberty, 1990
—UNHCR EXCOM Conclusions No.47 and No.59
—EU Resolution on Minimum Safeguards for Asylum Procedures, 1995

Other Guidelines
—"The Handbook on Procedures and Criteria for Determining Refugee Status," UNHCR, 1992
—UNHCR Policy on Refugee Children, 1993
—"Refugee Children—Guidelines on Protection and Care," UNHCR, 1992

Annex II
Children accompanied by adults who are not their parents
A. Principal caregivers
1.   In many cases the child will be accompanied by an adult caregiver who may or may not be a relative of the child. In order to determine whether

or not a child is considered unaccompanied, the following specific but non-exhaustive guidelines may assist in identifying and measuring the quality of the relationship between a child and a potential principal caregiver.

2.   Where a child is not with his/her parents in the first asylum country, then s/he will be, prima facie, unaccompanied.

3.   The attachment of a child to the refugee claim of an adult principal caregiver for the purpose of refugee status determination should only be made after a careful assessment of all known facts. Caution should be exercised when considering such a claim. The consequences of an erroneous judgement or an ill-advised finding that a child is accompanied by an adult principal caregiver for the purposes of refugee status determination under the principle of family unity are serious:

a) It may deprive the authority of the opportunity properly to investigate the child's history in the presentation of the refugee claim in an age-appropriate way;

b) It may prevent the authority from being alerted to the particular vulnerability and needs of the child and from assessing the best interest durable solution for the child once refugee status determination has been completed.

4.   If the interviewer is in doubt as to the veracity of the account presented or the nature of the relationship between caregiver and child, then the child should be processed as an unaccompanied child.

5.   Where a child is accompanied by an adult caregiver, the quality and durability of the relationship between the child and the caregiver must be evaluated to decide whether the presumption of "unaccompanied status" should be set aside. If, on evaluation of the nature of the relationship between the child and the caregiver, it is concluded that the child is not unaccompanied, then the child's case may be processed for refugee status under the regular status determination procedures with the adult caregiver according to the principle of family unity. (See paragraph 10)

6.   The primary parental responsibilities of a natural parent are the upbringing and development of the child to meet his/her fundamental needs (physical, psychological and spiritual requirements) in accordance with the child's rights under the Convention on the Rights of the Child. For cultural, social or other reasons, a child may not have been raised by his/her natural parents. If a child is in a first asylum country with an adult other than the natural parent but who has nevertheless assumed the principal caretaking responsibilities towards the child, then this arrangement should be respected even if it has not been legally formalised. In this respect, it should be noted that the terms "adoption" and "fostering" are sometimes used informally by custom in certain cultures and should not be confused with the legal use of such terms in industrialized countries. On the other hand, care should be exercised to ensure that the situation presented by the caregiver actually reflects the true relationship and is not open to abuse.

7.   As the primary caregiving responsibilities for the upbringing and development of a child usually rest with the natural parents, the competent authority should be satisfied that the natural parents of the child have entrusted caregiving responsibility to the accompanying adult principal caregiver. This adult principal caregiver should take full account of the longer-term consequence of taking on the responsibility for an extra child.

8.   The competent authority should also be satisfied that the principal caregiver has the maturity, commitment and expertise to adequately assume these responsibilities (i.e. the assumption of responsibility must be enduring and not simply transitory and will continue whatever the outcome of the refugee status determination procedure.) When meeting the basic needs of the family becomes a daily struggle, the child should not be put at risk of rejection, abandonment or exploitation by this adult caregiver.

9.   Where the child has been under the guidance of several de facto caregivers over a significant period during his/her upbringing in the country of origin, then the principal caregiver should be identified. Where the natural parents are included in this household structure, it may not be appropriate for the child to be attached to any other caregiver unless clear evidence is available that the natural parents had entrusted the

long term care of the child to another relative for reasons unrelated to the departure from the country of origin.

10.   If the principal caregiver is not recognized refugee status, "there is nothing to prevent any one of his dependants, if they can invoke reasons on their own account, from applying for recognition as refugees under the 1951 Convention or the 1967 Protocol relating to the Status of Refugees. The principle of family unity operates in favour of dependents, and not against them." Therefore, the substance of a child's circumstances should be evaluated for refugee status even if the child forms part of a family unit.

B. Adult siblings

1.   A child accompanied by an adult sibling should be processed with that sibling through the refugee status determination procedure on the presumption that:

a) they have a shared or common history and;

b) the adult sibling is aware of and able to articulate the child's claim for refugee status.

2.   If evidence suggests that the assumption of similar backgrounds is not valid or the adult sibling is not capable of articulating the child's claim for refugee status on his/her behalf then the child should be treated as an unaccompanied child for the purposes of his/her refugee status determination procedures. These should then be followed by an assessment of the durable solution in the 'best interests' of the child.

3.   The option of review to assess the durable solution in the best interests of each child should remain open, even if their cases have been processed together for refugee status determination. It should be a fluid rather than a static process which reflects the evolving nature of a child's legal or personal circumstances. If the background is shared and leads to a determination that the child and the adult sibling are refugees, then the durable solution for both will be either local integration or resettlement in the third country.

APPENDIX C
U.N. RULES FOR THE PROTECTION OF
JUVENILES DEPRIVED OF THEIR LIBERTY

United Nations Rules for the Protection of Juveniles Deprived of their Liberty, G.A. res. 45/113, annex, 45 U.N. GAOR Supp. (No. 49A) at 205, U.N. Doc. A/45/49 (1990).

I. Fundamental perspectives

1.   The juvenile justice system should uphold the rights and safety and promote the physical and mental well-being of juveniles. Imprisonment should be used as a last resort.

2.   Juveniles should only be deprived of their liberty in accordance with the principles and procedures set forth in these Rules and in the United Nations Standard Minimum Rules for the Administration of Juvenile Justice (The Beijing Rules). Deprivation of the liberty of a juvenile should be a disposition of last resort and for the minimum necessary period and should be limited to exceptional cases. The length of the sanction should be determined by the judicial authority, without precluding the possibility of his or her early release.

3.   The Rules are intended to establish minimum standards accepted by the United Nations for the protection of juveniles deprived of their liberty in all forms, consistent with human rights and fundamental freedoms, and with a view to counteracting the detrimental effects of all types of detention and to fostering integration in society.

4.   The Rules should be applied impartially, without discrimination of any kind as to race, color, sex, age, language, religion, nationality, political or other opinion, cultural beliefs or practices, property, birth or family status, ethnic or social origin, and disability. The religious and cultural beliefs, practices and moral concepts of the juvenile should be respected.

5.   The Rules are designed to serve as convenient standards of reference and to provide encouragement and guidance to professionals involved in the management of the juvenile justice system.

6.   The Rules should be made readily available to juvenile justice personnel in their national languages. Juveniles who are not fluent in the language

95

spoken by the personnel of the detention facility should have the right to the services of an interpreter free of charge whenever necessary, in particular during medical examinations and disciplinary proceedings.

7.   Where appropriate, States should incorporate the Rules into their legislation or amend it accordingly and provide effective remedies for their breach, including compensation when injuries are inflicted on juveniles. States should also monitor the application of the Rules.

8.   The competent authorities should constantly seek to increase the awareness of the public that the care of detained juveniles and preparation for their return to society is a social service of great importance, and to this end active steps should be taken to foster open contacts between the juveniles and the local community.

9.   Nothing in the Rules should be interpreted as precluding the application of the relevant United Nations and human rights instruments and standards, recognized by the international community, that are more conducive to ensuring the rights, care and protection of juveniles, children and all young persons.

10.   In the event that the practical application of particular Rules contained in sections II to V, inclusive, presents any conflict with the Rules contained in the present section, compliance with the latter shall be regarded as the predominant requirement.

II. Scope and application of the rules
11.   For the purposes of the Rules, the following definitions should apply:

(a) A juvenile is every person under the age of 18. The age limit below which it should not be permitted to deprive a child of his or her liberty should be determined by law;

(b) The deprivation of liberty means any form of detention or imprisonment or the placement of a person in a public or private custodial setting, from which this person is not permitted to leave at will, by order of any judicial, administrative or other public authority.

12.   The deprivation of liberty should be effected in conditions and circumstances which ensure respect for the human rights of juveniles. Juveniles detained in facilities should be guaranteed the benefit of meaningful activities and programmes which would serve to promote and sustain their health and self-respect, to foster their sense of responsibility and encourage those attitudes and skills that will assist them in developing their potential as members of society.

13.   Juveniles deprived of their liberty shall not for any reason related to their status be denied the civil, economic, political, social or cultural rights to which they are entitled under national or international law, and which are compatible with the deprivation of liberty.

14.   The protection of the individual rights of juveniles with special regard to the legality of the execution of the detention measures shall be ensured by the competent authority, while the objectives of social integration should be secured by regular inspections and other means of control carried out, according to international standards, national laws and regulations, by a duly constituted body authorized to visit the juveniles and not belonging to the detention facility.

15.   The Rules apply to all types and forms of detention facilities in which juveniles are deprived of their liberty. Sections I, II, IV and V of the Rules apply to all detention facilities and institutional settings in which juveniles are detained, and section III applies specifically to juveniles under arrest or awaiting trial.

16.   The Rules shall be implemented in the context of the economic, social and cultural conditions prevailing in each Member State.

III. Juveniles under arrest or awaiting trial

17.   Juveniles who are detained under arrest or awaiting trial ("untried") are presumed innocent and shall be treated as such. Detention before trial shall be avoided to the extent possible and limited to exceptional circumstances. Therefore, all efforts shall be made to apply alternative measures. When preventive detention is nevertheless used, juvenile courts and investigative bodies shall give the highest priority to the most expeditious processing of such cases to ensure the shortest possible

duration of detention. Untried detainees should be separated from convicted juveniles.

18.   The conditions under which an untried juvenile is detained should be consistent with the rules set out below, with additional specific provisions as are necessary and appropriate, given the requirements of the presumption of innocence, the duration of the detention and the legal status and circumstances of the juvenile. These provisions would include, but not necessarily be restricted to, the following:

a) Juveniles should have the right of legal counsel and be enabled to apply for free legal aid, where such aid is available, and to communicate regularly with their legal advisers. Privacy and confidentiality shall be ensured for such communications;

b) Juveniles should be provided, where possible, with opportunities to pursue work, with remuneration, and continue education or training, but should not be required to do so. Work, education or training should not cause the continuation of the detention;

c) Juveniles should receive and retain materials for their leisure and recreation as are compatible with the interests of the administration of justice.

IV. The management of juvenile facilities
A. Records

19.   All reports, including legal records, medical records and records of disciplinary proceedings, and all other documents relating to the form, content and details of treatment, should be placed in a confidential individual file, which should be kept up to date, accessible only to authorized persons and classified in such a way as to be easily understood. Where possible, every juvenile should have the right to contest any fact or opinion contained in his or her file so as to permit rectification of inaccurate, unfounded or unfair statements. In order to exercise this right, there should be procedures that allow an appropriate third party to have access to and to consult the file on request. Upon release, the records of juveniles shall be sealed, and, at an appropriate time, expunged.

20.   No juvenile should be received in any detention facility without a valid commitment order of a judicial, administrative or other public authority. The details of this order should be immediately entered in the register. No juvenile should be detained in any facility where there is no such register.

B. *Admission, registration, movement and transfer*

21.   In every place where juveniles are detained, a complete and secure record of the following information should be kept concerning each juvenile received:

a) Information on the identity of the juvenile;

b) The fact of and reasons for commitment and the authority therefor;

c) The day and hour of admission, transfer and release;

d) Details of the notifications to parents and guardians on every admission, transfer or release of the juvenile in their care at the time of commitment;

e) Details of known physical and mental health problems, including drug and alcohol abuse.

22.   The information on admission, place, transfer and release should be provided without delay to the parents and guardians or closest relative of the juvenile concerned.

23.   As soon as possible after reception, full reports and relevant information on the personal situation and circumstances of each juvenile should be drawn up and submitted to the administration.

24.   On admission, all juveniles shall be given a copy of the rules governing the detention facility and a written description of their rights and obligations in a language they can understand, together with the address of the authorities competent to receive complaints, as well as the address of public or private agencies and organizations which provide legal assistance. For those juveniles who are illiterate or who cannot understand the language in the written form, the information should be conveyed in a manner enabling full comprehension.

25.   All juveniles should be helped to understand the regulations governing the internal organization of the facility, the goals and methodology of the care provided, the disciplinary requirements and procedures, other authorized methods of seeking information and of making complaints and all such other matters as are necessary to enable them to understand fully their rights and obligations during detention.

26.   The transport of juveniles should be carried out at the expense of the administration in conveyances with adequate ventilation and light, in conditions that should in no way subject them to hardship or indignity. Juveniles should not be transferred from one facility to another arbitrarily.

C. Classification and placement

27.   As soon as possible after the moment of admission, each juvenile should be interviewed, and a psychological and social report identifying any factors relevant to the specific type and level of care and programme required by the juvenile should be prepared. This report, together with the report prepared by a medical officer who has examined the juvenile upon admission, should be forwarded to the director for purposes of determining the most appropriate placement for the juvenile within the facility and the specific type and level of care and programme required and to be pursued. When special rehabilitative treatment is required, and the length of stay in the facility permits, trained personnel of the facility should prepare a written, individualized treatment plan specifying treatment objectives and time-frame and the means, stages and delays with which the objectives should be approached.

28.   The detention of juveniles should only take place under conditions that take full account of their particular needs, status and special requirements according to their age, personality, sex and type of offense, as well as mental and physical health, and which ensure their protection from harmful influences and risk situations. The principal criterion for the separation of different categories of juveniles deprived of their liberty should be the provision of the type of care best suited to the particular needs of the individuals concerned and the protection of their physical, mental and moral integrity and well-being.

29.   In all detention facilities juveniles should be separated from adults, unless they are members of the same family. Under controlled conditions,

juveniles may be brought together with carefully selected adults as part of a special programme that has been shown to be beneficial for the juveniles concerned.

30. Open detention facilities for juveniles should be established. Open detention facilities are those with no or minimal security measures. The population in such detention facilities should be as small as possible. The number of juveniles detained in closed facilities should be small enough to enable individualized treatment. Detention facilities for juveniles should be decentralized and of such size as to facilitate access and contact between the juveniles and their families. Small-scale detention facilities should be established and integrated into the social, economic and cultural environment of the community.

D. Physical environment and accommodation

31. Juveniles deprived of their liberty have the right to facilities and services that meet all the requirements of health and human dignity.

32. The design of detention facilities for juveniles and the physical environment should be in keeping with the rehabilitative aim of residential treatment, with due regard to the need of the juvenile for privacy, sensory stimuli, opportunities for association with peers and participation in sports, physical exercise and leisure-time activities. The design and structure of juvenile detention facilities should be such as to minimize the risk of fire and to ensure safe evacuation from the premises. There should be an effective alarm system in case of fire, as well as formal and drilled procedures to ensure the safety of the juveniles. Detention facilities should not be located in areas where there are known health or other hazards or risks.

33. Sleeping accommodation should normally consist of small group dormitories or individual bedrooms, while bearing in mind local standards. During sleeping hours there should be regular, unobtrusive supervision of all sleeping areas, including individual rooms and group dormitories, in order to ensure the protection of each juvenile. Every juvenile should, in accordance with local or national standards, be provided with separate and sufficient bedding, which should be clean when issued, kept in good order and changed often enough to ensure cleanliness.

34.   Sanitary installations should be so located and of a sufficient standard to enable every juvenile to comply, as required, with their physical needs in privacy and in a clean and decent manner.

35.   The possession of personal effects is a basic element of the right to privacy and essential to the psychological well-being of the juvenile. The right of every juvenile to possess personal effects and to have adequate storage facilities for them should be fully recognized and respected. Personal effects that the juvenile does not choose to retain or that are confiscated should be placed in safe custody. An inventory thereof should be signed by the juvenile. Steps should be taken to keep them in good condition. All such articles and money should be returned to the juvenile on release, except in so far as he or she has been authorized to spend money or send such property out of the facility. If a juvenile receives or is found in possession of any medicine, the medical officer should decide what use should be made of it.

36.   To the extent possible juveniles should have the right to use their own clothing. Detention facilities should ensure that each juvenile has personal clothing suitable for the climate and adequate to ensure good health, and which should in no manner be degrading or humiliating. Juveniles removed from or leaving a facility for any purpose should be allowed to wear their own clothing.

37.   Every detention facility shall ensure that every juvenile receives food that is suitably prepared and presented at normal meal times and of a quality and quantity to satisfy the standards of dietetics, hygiene and health and, as far as possible, religious and cultural requirements. Clean drinking water should be available to every juvenile at any time.

E. Education, vocational training and work

38.   Every juvenile of compulsory school age has the right to education suited to his or her needs and abilities and designed to prepare him or her for return to society. Such education should be provided outside the detention facility in community schools wherever possible and, in any case, by qualified teachers through programmes integrated with the education system of the country so that, after release, juveniles may continue their education without difficulty. Special attention should be given by the administration of the detention facilities to the education of juveniles of

foreign origin or with particular cultural or ethnic needs. Juveniles who are illiterate or have cognitive or learning difficulties should have the right to special education.

39.   Juveniles above compulsory school age who wish to continue their education should be permitted and encouraged to do so, and every effort should be made to provide them with access to appropriate educational programmes.

40.   Diplomas or educational certificates awarded to juveniles while in detention should not indicate in any way that the juvenile has been institutionalized.

41.   Every detention facility should provide access to a library that is adequately stocked with both instructional and recreational books and periodicals suitable for the juveniles, who should be encouraged and enabled to make full use of it.

42.   Every juvenile should have the right to receive vocational training in occupations likely to prepare him or her for future employment.

43.   With due regard to proper vocational selection and to the requirements of institutional administration, juveniles should be able to choose the type of work they wish to perform.

44.   All protective national and international standards applicable to child labor and young workers should apply to juveniles deprived of their liberty.

45.   Wherever possible, juveniles should be provided with the opportunity to perform remunerated labor, if possible within the local community, as a complement to the vocational training provided in order to enhance the possibility of finding suitable employment when they return to their communities. The type of work should be such as to provide appropriate training that will be of benefit to the juveniles following release. The organization and methods of work offered in detention facilities should resemble as closely as possible those of similar work in the community, so as to prepare juveniles for the conditions of normal occupational life.

46.   Every juvenile who performs work should have the right to an equitable remuneration. The interests of the juveniles and of their vocational training should not be subordinated to the purpose of making a profit for the detention facility or a third party. Part of the earnings of a juvenile should normally be set aside to constitute a savings fund to be handed over to the juvenile on release. The juvenile should have the right to use the remainder of those earnings to purchase articles for his or her own use or to indemnify the victim injured by his or her offense or to send it to his or her family or other persons outside the detention facility.

F. Recreation

47.   Every juvenile should have the right to a suitable amount of time for daily free exercise, in the open air whenever weather permits, during which time appropriate recreational and physical training should normally be provided. Adequate space, installations and equipment should be provided for these activities. Every juvenile should have additional time for daily leisure activities, part of which should be devoted, if the juvenile so wishes, to arts and crafts skill development. The detention facility should ensure that each juvenile is physically able to participate in the available programmes of physical education. Remedial physical education and therapy should be offered, under medical supervision, to juveniles needing it.

G. Religion

48.   Every juvenile should be allowed to satisfy the needs of his or her religious and spiritual life, in particular by attending the services or meetings provided in the detention facility or by conducting his or her own services and having possession of the necessary books or items of religious observance and instruction of his or her denomination. If a detention facility contains a sufficient number of juveniles of a given religion, one or more qualified representatives of that religion should be appointed or approved and allowed to hold regular services and to pay pastoral visits in private to juveniles at their request. Every juvenile should have the right to receive visits from a qualified representative of any religion of his or her choice, as well as the right not to participate in religious services and freely to decline religious education, counseling or indoctrination.

H. Medical care

49.   Every juvenile shall receive adequate medical care, both preventive and remedial, including dental, ophthalmological and mental health care, as well as pharmaceutical products and special diets as medically indicated. All such medical care should, where possible, be provided to detained juveniles through the appropriate health facilities and services of the community in which the detention facility is located, in order to prevent stigmatization of the juvenile and promote self-respect and integration into the community.

50.   Every juvenile has a right to be examined by a physician immediately upon admission to a detention facility, for the purpose of recording any evidence of prior ill-treatment and identifying any physical or mental condition requiring medical attention.

51.   The medical services provided to juveniles should seek to detect and should treat any physical or mental illness, substance abuse or other condition that may hinder the integration of the juvenile into society. Every detention facility for juveniles should have immediate access to adequate medical facilities and equipment appropriate to the number and requirements of its residents and staff trained in preventive health care and the handling of medical emergencies. Every juvenile who is ill, who complains of illness or who demonstrates symptoms of physical or mental difficulties, should be examined promptly by a medical officer.

52.   Any medical officer who has reason to believe that the physical or mental health of a juvenile has been or will be injuriously affected by continued detention, a hunger strike or any condition of detention should report this fact immediately to the director of the detention facility in question and to the independent authority responsible for safeguarding the well-being of the juvenile.

53.   A juvenile who is suffering from mental illness should be treated in a specialized institution under independent medical management. Steps should be taken, by arrangement with appropriate agencies, to ensure any necessary continuation of mental health care after release.

54.   Juvenile detention facilities should adopt specialized drug abuse prevention and rehabilitation programmes administered by qualified

personnel. These programmes should be adapted to the age, sex and other requirements of the juveniles concerned, and detoxification facilities and services staffed by trained personnel should be available to drug- or alcohol-dependent juveniles.

55.   Medicines should be administered only for necessary treatment on medical grounds and, when possible, after having obtained the informed consent of the juvenile concerned. In particular, they must not be administered with a view to eliciting information or a confession, as a punishment or as a means of restraint. Juveniles shall never be testers in the experimental use of drugs and treatment. The administration of any drug should always be authorized and carried out by qualified medical personnel.

I. Notification of illness, injury and death

56.   The family or guardian of a juvenile and any other person designated by the juvenile have the right to be informed of the state of health of the juvenile on request and in the event of any important changes in the health of the juvenile. The director of the detention facility should notify immediately the family or guardian of the juvenile concerned, or other designated person, in case of death, illness requiring transfer of the juvenile to an outside medical facility, or a condition requiring clinical care within the detention facility for more than 48 hours. Notification should also be given to the consular authorities of the State of which a foreign juvenile is a citizen.

57.   Upon the death of a juvenile during the period of deprivation of liberty, the nearest relative should have the right to inspect the death certificate, see the body and determine the method of disposal of the body. Upon the death of a juvenile in detention, there should be an independent inquiry into the causes of death, the report of which should be made accessible to the nearest relative. This inquiry should also be made when the death of a juvenile occurs within six months from the date of his or her release from the detention facility and there is reason to believe that the death is related to the period of detention.

58.   A juvenile should be informed at the earliest possible time of the death, serious illness or injury of any immediate family member and should be

provided with the opportunity to attend the funeral of the deceased or go to the bedside of a critically ill relative.

J. Contacts with the wider community

59.   Every means should be provided to ensure that juveniles have adequate communication with the outside world, which is an integral part of the right to fair and humane treatment and is essential to the preparation of juveniles for their return to society. Juveniles should be allowed to communicate with their families, friends and other persons or representatives of reputable outside organizations, to leave detention facilities for a visit to their home and family and to receive special permission to leave the detention facility for educational, vocational or other important reasons. Should the juvenile be serving a sentence, the time spent outside a detention facility should be counted as part of the period of sentence.

60.   Every juvenile should have the right to receive regular and frequent visits, in principle once a week and not less than once a month, in circumstances that respect the need of the juvenile for privacy, contact and unrestricted communication with the family and the defense counsel.

61.   Every juvenile should have the right to communicate in writing or by telephone at least twice a week with the person of his or her choice, unless legally restricted, and should be assisted as necessary in order effectively to enjoy this right. Every juvenile should have the right to receive correspondence.

62.   Juveniles should have the opportunity to keep themselves informed regularly of the news by reading newspapers, periodicals and other publications, through access to radio and television programmes and motion pictures, and through the visits of the representatives of any lawful club or organization in which the juvenile is interested.

K. Limitations of physical restraint and the use of force

63.   Recourse to instruments of restraint and to force for any purpose should be prohibited, except as set forth in rule 64 below.

64.   Instruments of restraint and force can only be used in exceptional cases, where all other control methods have been exhausted and failed, and only

as explicitly authorized and specified by law and regulation. They should not cause humiliation or degradation, and should be used restrictively and only for the shortest possible period of time. By order of the director of the administration, such instruments might be resorted to in order to prevent the juvenile from inflicting self-injury, injuries to others or serious destruction of property. In such instances, the director should at once consult medical and other relevant personnel and report to the higher administrative authority.

65.   The carrying and use of weapons by personnel should be prohibited in any facility where juveniles are detained.

L. Disciplinary procedures

66.   Any disciplinary measures and procedures should maintain the interest of safety and an ordered community life and should be consistent with the upholding of the inherent dignity of the juvenile and the fundamental objective of institutional care, namely, instilling a sense of justice, self-respect and respect for the basic rights of every person.

67.   All disciplinary measures constituting cruel, inhuman or degrading treatment shall be strictly prohibited, including corporal punishment, placement in a dark cell, closed or solitary confinement or any other punishment that may compromise the physical or mental health of the juvenile concerned. The reduction of diet and the restriction or denial of contact with family members should be prohibited for any purpose. Labor should always be viewed as an educational tool and a means of promoting the self-respect of the juvenile in preparing him or her for return to the community and should not be imposed as a disciplinary sanction. No juvenile should be sanctioned more than once for the same disciplinary infraction. Collective sanctions should be prohibited.

68.   Legislation or regulations adopted by the competent administrative authority should establish norms concerning the following, taking full account of the fundamental characteristics, needs and rights of juveniles:

a) Conduct constituting a disciplinary offense;
b) Type and duration of disciplinary sanctions that may be inflicted;
c) The authority competent to impose such sanctions;
d) The authority competent to consider appeals.

69.   A report of misconduct should be presented promptly to the competent authority, which should decide on it without undue delay. The competent authority should conduct a thorough examination of the case.

70.   No juvenile should be disciplinarily sanctioned except in strict accordance with the terms of the law and regulations in force. No juvenile should be sanctioned unless he or she has been informed of the alleged infraction in a manner appropriate to the full understanding of the juvenile, and given a proper opportunity of presenting his or her defense, including the right of appeal to a competent impartial authority. Complete records should be kept of all disciplinary proceedings.

71.   No juveniles should be responsible for disciplinary functions except in the supervision of specified social, educational or sports activities or in self-government programmes.

M. Inspection and complaints

72.   Qualified inspectors or an equivalent duly constituted authority not belonging to the administration of the facility should be empowered to conduct inspections on a regular basis and to undertake unannounced inspections on their own initiative, and should enjoy full guarantees of independence in the exercise of this function. Inspectors should have unrestricted access to all persons employed by or working in any facility where juveniles are or may be deprived of their liberty, to all juveniles and to all records of such facilities.

73.   Qualified medical officers attached to the inspecting authority or the public health service should participate in the inspections, evaluating compliance with the rules concerning the physical environment, hygiene, accommodation, food, exercise and medical services, as well as any other aspect or conditions of institutional life that affect the physical and mental health of juveniles. Every juvenile should have the right to talk in confidence to any inspecting officer.

74.   After completing the inspection, the inspector should be required to submit a report on the findings. The report should include an evaluation of the compliance of the detention facilities with the present rules and relevant provisions of national law, and recommendations regarding any steps considered necessary to ensure compliance with them. Any facts

discovered by an inspector that appear to indicate that a violation of legal provisions concerning the rights of juveniles or the operation of a juvenile detention facility has occurred should be communicated to the competent authorities for investigation and prosecution.

75.   Every juvenile should have the opportunity of making requests or complaints to the director of the detention facility and to his or her authorized representative.

76.   Every juvenile should have the right to make a request or complaint, without censorship as to substance, to the central administration, the judicial authority or other proper authorities through approved channels, and to be informed of the response without delay.

77.   Efforts should be made to establish an independent office (ombudsman) to receive and investigate complaints made by juveniles deprived of their liberty and to assist in the achievement of equitable settlements.

78.   Every juvenile should have the right to request assistance from family members, legal counselors, humanitarian groups or others where possible, in order to make a complaint. Illiterate juveniles should be provided with assistance should they need to use the services of public or private agencies and organizations which provide legal counsel or which are competent to receive complaints.

N. Return to the community

79.   All juveniles should benefit from arrangements designed to assist them in returning to society, family life, education or employment after release. Procedures, including early release, and special courses should be devised to this end.

80.   Competent authorities should provide or ensure services to assist juveniles in re-establishing themselves in society and to lessen prejudice against such juveniles. These services should ensure', to the extent possible, that the juvenile is provided with suitable residence, employment, clothing, and sufficient means to maintain himself or herself upon release in order to facilitate successful reintegration. The representatives of agencies providing such services should be consulted and should have access to

juveniles while detained, with a view to assisting them in their return to the community.

V. Personnel

81.   Personnel should be qualified and include a sufficient number of specialists such as educators, vocational instructors, counselors, social workers, psychiatrists and psychologists. These and other specialist staff should normally be employed on a permanent basis. This should not preclude part-time or volunteer workers when the level of support and training they can provide is appropriate and beneficial. Detention facilities should make use of all remedial, educational, moral, spiritual, and other resources and forms of assistance that are appropriate and available in the community, according to the individual needs and problems of detained juveniles.

82.   The administration should provide for the careful selection and recruitment of every grade and type of personnel, since the proper management of detention facilities depends on their integrity, humanity, ability and professional capacity to deal with juveniles, as well as personal suitability for the work.

83.   To secure the foregoing ends, personnel should be appointed as professional officers with adequate remuneration to attract and retain suitable women and men. The personnel of juvenile detention facilities should be continually encouraged to fulfil their duties and obligations in a humane, committed, professional, fair and efficient manner, to conduct themselves at all times in such a way as to deserve and gain the respect of the juveniles, and to provide juveniles with a positive role model and perspective.

84.   The administration should introduce forms of organization and management that facilitate communications between different categories of staff in each detention facility so as to enhance cooperation between the various services engaged in the care of juveniles, as well as between staff and the administration, with a view to ensuring that staff directly in contact with juveniles are able to function in conditions favorable to the efficient fulfilment of their duties.

85.   The personnel should receive such training as will enable them to carry out their responsibilities effectively, in particular training in child psychology, child welfare and international standards and norms of human rights and the rights of the child, including the present Rules. The personnel should maintain and improve their knowledge and professional capacity by attending courses of in-service training, to be organized at suitable intervals throughout their career.

86.   The director of a facility should be adequately qualified for his or her task, with administrative ability and suitable training and experience, and should carry out his or her duties on a full-time basis.

87.   In the performance of their duties, personnel of detention facilities should respect and protect the human dignity and fundamental human rights of all juveniles, in particular, as follows:

a) No member of the detention facility or institutional personnel may inflict, instigate or tolerate any act of torture or any form of harsh, cruel, inhuman or degrading treatment, punishment, correction or discipline under any pretext or circumstance whatsoever;

b) All personnel should rigorously oppose and combat any act of corruption, reporting it without delay to the competent authorities;

c) All personnel should respect the present Rules. Personnel who have reason to believe that a serious violation of the present Rules has occurred or is about to occur should report the matter to their superior authorities or organs vested with reviewing or remedial power;

d) All personnel should ensure the full protection of the physical and mental health of juveniles, including protection from physical, sexual and emotional abuse and exploitation, and should take immediate action to secure medical attention whenever required;

e) All personnel should respect the right of the juvenile to privacy, and, in particular, should safeguard all confidential matters concerning juveniles or their families learned as a result of their professional capacity;

f) All personnel should seek to minimize any differences between life inside and outside the detention facility which tend to lessen due respect for the dignity of juveniles as human beings.

APPENDIX D
SELECTED ARTICLES FROM ALIEN MINORS SHELTER
CARE PROGRAM GUIDELINES AND REQUIREMENTS

I. Introduction

In 1987, the United States Department of Justice (DOJ), Community Relations Service (CRS), and the Immigration and Naturalization Service (INS) entered into an agreement to establish a network of community based shelter care programs to provide physical care and maintenance and other child welfare related services to alien minors detained in the custody of the INS.

This CRS Alien Minors Shelter Care Program (AMSCP) provides a safe and appropriate environment for minors during the interim period beginning when the minor is transferred into a CRS AMSCP and ending when a minor is released from custody by the INS or removed from the United States.

This document provides operational policy instructions to current AMSCP vendors and application guidance to agencies and organizations applying for Federal funds to develop plans, programs, and administrative procedures for the care and maintenance of alien minors held in the custody of the INS.

II. Background

The CRS Shelter Care Program described in this document was developed as an inter-agency approach and response to the complex issues associated with the apprehension and detention of alien minors by the INS.

The United States has traditionally accepted immigrants and refugees from around the world. Ordinarily, persons desiring such status apply for entry while residing in their own country or in a third country known as a "country of first asylum." However, minors unaccompanied by adult relatives have been entering the United States since 1978 without any prior administrative processing.

Since 1980, the CRS has provided temporary shelter care and other related services to Cuban/Haitian entrants and other alien unaccompanied minors apprehended and detained by the INS in South Florida and Texas. These minors are provided physical care and maintenance and other services while awaiting disposition of various INS proceedings. This CRS program has provided services to over 8,500 minors apprehended by the INS.

Since 1987, significant numbers of minors have been entering the United States at various border points between the United States and Mexico. The largest concentrations of entries are in the States of Texas and California. These minors have traditionally come from El Salvador, Nicaragua, Guatemala, and Honduras. But today minors are coming from many other countries. When apprehended by Federal authorities, these minors are taken to an INS district office or Border Patrol office. The INS requires that minors be released or transferred to an appropriate child care facility within 72 hours of apprehension.

Many of these unaccompanied minors (primarily males 15 to 17 years of age) are "bound for" parents, other relatives, godparents, or friends already residing in the United States. Many of them may also be attempting to establish residence in this country.

In 1987, the CRS and the INS entered into a comprehensive Inter-Agency Agreement which provided the framework for a national initiative to address the challenges and complex issues created by this influx of mainly Central American youth. Since that year, more than 6,000 alien unaccompanied minors have received shelter care and other child welfare services.

Since 1991, there have been increasing numbers of alien minors apprehended at airports and on both coasts of the United States.

In 1993, the CRS further expanded its existing network of services to include the provision of shelter care, family reunification, and foster care services to Chinese unaccompanied minors held in the legal custody of the INS.

The CRS works closely with Cooperative Agreement Recipients (hereafter referred to as Recipients) to assist with the development and administration of programs that address the intricate and complex needs of these youth for care and protection in a manner which meets the mandates of current United States law.

III. Scope of work

Recipients shall provide temporary shelter care and other related services to alien minors who have been referred to them by the INS or the CRS. Shelter care services will be provided for the interim period beginning when the minor is placed in the Shelter Care Program and ending when the INS releases the minor from custody, transfers him or her to another facility, or removes him or her for the United States.

These minors, although placed in the physical custody of the CRS Recipient, remain in the legal custody of the INS.

The population level of alien minors is expected to fluctuate. Program content must, therefore, reflect differential planning of services for minors in various stages of personal adjustment and administrative processing. Although the population of minors is projected to consist primarily of adolescents, Recipients are expected to be able to serve some children 12 years of age and younger.

Recipients are expected to facilitate the provision of assistance and services for each alien minor including, but not limited to: physical care and maintenance, access to routine and emergency medical care, comprehensive needs assessment, education, recreation, individual and group counseling, access to religious services, and other social services. Recipients may be required to assist in family reunification efforts. Other services that are necessary and appropriate for these minors may be provided if CRS determines in advance that the service is reasonable and necessary for a particular child.

Recipients are expected to develop and implement an appropriate individualized service plan for the care and maintenance of each minor in accordance with his or her needs as determined in an intake assessment. In addition, Recipients are required to implement and administer a case management system which tracks and monitors each minor's progress on a regular basis to ensure that he or she receives the full range of program services in an integrated and comprehensive manner.

Shelter care services shall be provided in accordance with applicable State child welfare statutes and generally accepted child welfare standards, practices, principals, and procedures. *ALL PROGRAMS MUST BE LICENSED UNDER APPLICABLE STATE LAW.*

The CRS intends that services be delivered in an open type of setting, i.e., without security fences and security hardware or other major restraining construction typically associated with correctional facilities. However, Recipients *are required* to structure programs and implement strategies designed to discourage runaways, prevent the unauthorized absence of minors in care, and protect against influences which may jeopardize the well-being of the minor.

Delivery of this service is to be accomplished in a manner which is sensitive to culture, native language, and the complex needs of these minors.

VIII. Definition of alien minors

An alien minor is defined as a male or female foreign national under 18 years of age who is detained in the custody of the INS and is the subject of exclusion or deportation proceedings under the Immigration and Nationality Act (INA). Many alien minors, when apprehended by the INS, are not accompanied by a family member, such as a parent, grandparent, adult sibling, aunt or uncle.

IX. Client population

It is anticipated that the client population will generally consist of males, 15-17 years of age. Females comprise approximately 15% of the total population of alien minors. These minors are primarily nationals of El Salvador, Nicaragua, Guatemala, Honduras, Mexico, and the Peoples Republic of China; however, Recipients can expect to provide services to significant numbers of minors from other countries. Recipients must also be prepared to provide child-care services to limited numbers of minors 12 years of age and younger.

Clients will generally be dependent children without significant behavioral or psychological problems. However, many minors have inconsistent or sporadic educational histories and some may be illiterate in their own language.

X. Program design

Shelter care and related services can be provided through either residential, foster, or group care programs. The ability to provide a mix of services and deliver these services in geographic proximity to the applicable INS District Office is highly desirable due to the varying needs of the minors, the needs of the Federal Government, and the varying length of time that the minors will be in care.

Recipients must be able to admit and discharge minors on a 24 hour per day, seven (7) day a week basis.

Control, predictability, and accountability are essential elements of a successful program. A highly structured, active, and productive program of activities mitigates against disruptive behavior.

Program design must ensure that the minors follow an integrated and structured daily routine which shall include, but not limited to: education, recreation, vocational experiences or chores, study period, counseling , group interaction, free time, and access to religious and legal services.

This daily routine will enhance programmatic supervision and accountability as well as encourage the development of individual and social responsibility on the part of each minor. Program rules and disciplinary procedures must be written and translated into Spanish, or a language understood by the minor. These rules must be provided to the minors and fully understood by each minor and all program staff.

Most minors served by this program are individuals who are alleged to have entered or attempted to enter the United States in violation of law. Some minors may have committed a deportable act after lawful entry. Others may be referred to the INS by State or local law enforcement officials. These minors may be seeking some type of relief from deportation through an administrative process.

The length of care per minor is anticipated to be less that thirty (30) days; however, due to the variables and uncertainties inherent in each case, Recipients must design programs which are able to provide a combination of short-term and long-term care.

Rights of minors

Each minor is to enjoy a reasonable right to privacy, which shall include the right to (a) wear his or her own clothes, when available; (b) retain a private space in the residential facility, group, or foster home for the storage of personal belongings; (c) talk privately on the phone, as permitted by the house rules and regulations; (d) visit privately with guests, as permitted by the house rules and regulations; and (e) receive and send uncensored mail unless there is a reasonable belief that the mail contains contraband. Contraband is any item possessed by minors or found within the facility that is illegal by law or that is expressly prohibited by those legally charged with the responsibility for administering and operating the facility.

Recipients shall have a written policy and procedure that will provide each minor freedom from discrimination based on race, religion, national origin, sex, handicap, or political beliefs, and ensures equal access to various services and work assignments, as appropriate.

Recipients shall ensure that all minors have equal opportunities to participate in all activities and receive all services offered by the program. Work assignments and all administrative decisions likewise will be made without discrimination.

Recipients shall assist minors in making confidential contact with attorneys and their authorized representatives. Contact will include but is not limited to, telephone communications, uncensored correspondence, and visits. An accurate and current reference list of voluntary agencies and attorneys who provide services without compensation will be posted and provided to all minors.

Recipients shall make reasonable efforts to ensure that minors are able to participate in religious services of their choice and religious counseling on a voluntary basis. Reasonable provisions shall be made by the staff to adhere to dietary and other requirements of various faiths. Recipients shall ensure that minors are not subjected to corporal punishment, humiliation, mental abuse, or punitive interference with the daily functions of living, such as eating or sleeping. Any sanctions employed shall not:

- Adversely affect either a minor's health, or physical or psychological well-being; or

- Deny minors regular meals, sufficient sleep, exercise, medical care, correspondence privileges, or legal assistance.

Each Recipient shall have written policy and procedures which ensure the rights of minors to have access to the courts.

Recipients shall have written procedures regarding chore sharing schedules. Minors are not required to participate in uncompensated work assignments unless the work is yard work or light housekeeping of the personal and common areas, or the work is part of an approved vocational training program.

XI. Program management
A. Organizational structure and coordination

Recipients are required to have operative plans which identify organizational structures, lines of authority, and lines of responsibility. Recipients are also required to maintain and administer comprehensive plans which facilitate and enhance intra-program and intra-organizational (if appropriate) communication. At a minimum, programs must ensure weekly staff meetings to discuss service plans, progress, and work schedules for each minor.

Recipients must maintain linkages with other social service agencies and the local District Office of the INS. The Program Director for each Recipient shall be responsible for maintaining working relationships and liaison with community organizations and the INS.